INTRODUCTION: WHY MOST BUDGETS FAIL (AND HOW THIS BOOK WILL MAKE YOURS SUCCEED)

Ah, budgeting. The financial equivalent of eating your vegetables or flossing your teeth.

We all know we should do it, but somehow it always ends up at the bottom of our to-do list, right next to "organize the garage" and "learn Esperanto." But, unlike those other neglected tasks, mastering the art of budgeting can actually improve your life.

And I'm not just talking about having a few extra bucks in your pocket (though that's certainly nice). I'm talking about the kind of financial freedom that let's you sleep soundly at night, pursue your dreams without constantly checking your bank balance, and maybe even splurge on that fancy coffee without a side order of guilt.

Now, I know what you're thinking. "But I've tried budgeting before, and it was about as fun as watching paint dry." Trust me, I've been there.

My first try at budgeting involved a complicated spreadsheet, three different colored pens, and a level of optimism that would make Pollyanna look like a pessimist.

Needless to say, it didn't last long. But that's the beauty of this book – we're going to approach budgeting in a way that actually works for real people living in the real world.

The thing is, most budgets fail for the same reason most diets fail – they're too restrictive, too complicated, and they don't account for the fact that we're human beings with wants, needs, and the occasional weakness for impulse purchases. (I'm looking at you, late-night Amazon shoppers.) But it doesn't have to be this way.

With the right approach, budgeting can be empowering, liberating, and dare I say it, even a little bit fun.

We're about to start on a financial journey that will change the way you think about money forever. And who knows?

(Okay, that might be a stretch, but stranger things have happened.)

Let's start by addressing the elephant in the room – why do most budgets fail? It's not because we're all secretly terrible with money or because we lack willpower.

Many traditional budgeting methods are set up for failure from the get-go.

They're often based on unrealistic expectations, ignore the psychological aspects of spending, and treat budgeting as a punishment rather than a tool for achieving our goals.

One of the biggest culprits is the "one-size-fits-all" approach. You know the type – those budgets that tell you to allocate exactly 30% for housing, 15% for transportation, and so on.

But, your life isn't a pie chart.

Maybe you live in a city with sky-high rent but save money by walking everywhere. Or perhaps you work from home but have a weakness for gourmet cooking ingredients.

A budget that doesn't reflect your unique circumstances and priorities is about as useful as a chocolate teapot.

Another common pitfall, problem, issue, problem, issue is the "all or nothing" mentality. We start our budgets with the best intentions, vowing to cut out all unnecessary expenses and live like financial monks. But then life happens.

Maybe you have an unexpected car repair, or your best friend announces a destination wedding. Suddenly, your carefully crafted budget is in tatters, and you're ready to throw in the towel entirely.

This is where flexibility becomes crucial – a good budget should be able to bend without breaking.

Then there's the issue of motivation. Tracking every penny you spend isn't exactly thrilling.

It's easy to start strong, diligently logging every purchase for the first week or two.

But as time goes on, the novelty wears off, and before you know it, you're back to your old spending habits. This is where the psychology of budgeting comes into play – we need to find ways to make the process engaging and rewarding in the long term.

But perhaps the most insidious reason budgets fail is that they often focus solely on restriction. It's all about what you can't do, what you can't buy, where you need to cut back.

And while controlling spending is certainly part of budgeting, it's not the whole story.
A truly effective budget should also be about empowerment – giving you the tools to achieve your financial goals, whatever they may be.

So, how does this book suggest to overcome these obstacles and turn you into a budgeting superstar? Well, I'm glad you asked.

(Okay, you didn't actually ask, but let's pretend you did .)

First and foremost, we're going to ditch the one-size-fits-all approach. Instead, we'll work on creating a personalized budget that reflects your unique circumstances, priorities, and goals.

I'm not talking about forcing your life to fit a pre-determined set of categories – this involves crafting a financial plan that actually makes sense for you.

We'll also tackle the psychological aspects of budgeting head-on. This means understanding the emotional factors that drive our spending decisions and developing strategies to work with our natural tendencies rather than against them.

Ever wonder why you can resist buying that new gadget for weeks, only to cave in at the first sign of stress?

We'll explore the science behind these behaviors and how to use them to our advantage.

Flexibility is going to be a key theme throughout this book. We'll learn how to create a budget that can adapt to life's inevitable curveballs without completely derailing our progress.

This includes building in buffer zones for unexpected expenses and learning how to make smart trade-offs when necessary.

But perhaps most importantly, we're going to shift the focus from restriction to empowerment. Yes, we'll talk about ways to cut unnecessary spending, but we'll also explore how to use your budget as a tool to fund the things that truly matter to you.

Whether that's saving for a dream vacation, starting your own business, or simply having the peace of mind that comes with a solid emergency fund, your budget should be working for you, not against you.

Now, I know what some of you might be thinking. "This all sounds great in theory, but how does it actually work in practice?" Well, my financially curious friend, I'm glad you asked.

Let's start with a real-world example. Meet Sarah, a 28-year-old graphic designer living in a busy city. Sarah had tried budgeting before, using one of those standard templates she found online.

It told her she should be spending no more than 30% of her income on rent. The problem?

In her high-cost city, even a tiny studio apartment ate up closer to 40% of her paycheck. Frustrated, she gave up on budgeting altogether, figuring it just wasn't possible in her situation.

But here's where our approach differs. Instead of trying to force Sarah's life to fit a pre-determined budget, we helped her create a plan that reflected her reality.

Yes, her housing costs were higher than the "ideal," but she saved money in other areas.

She worked from home most days, saving on transportation costs, and she was an avid cook, which kept her food expenses relatively low.

By acknowledging these factors and building them into her budget, Sarah was able to create a realistic plan that she could actually stick to. More importantly, she no longer felt like a failure for not meeting some arbitrary standard.

Her budget became a tool for managing her money, not a source of stress and guilt.

But creating a personalized budget is just the first step. The real magic happens when we start to dig into the psychology of spending and saving.

This is where things get really interesting (and where I get to show off all the fascinating research I've been nerding out over).

Did you know that simply changing the way you label your savings can have a significant impact on how likely you are to stick to your budget? A study published in the Journal of Marketing Research found that people were more likely to save money when they gave their savings accounts specific labels (like "Hawaii Vacation Fund" or "Dream Home Down Payment") rather than generic ones like "Savings Account."

This makes use of a psychological principle known as mental accounting. Essentially, our brains treat money differently depending on how we categorize it.

When we give our savings a specific purpose, it becomes more "real" to us, and we're less likely to dip into it for other expenses.

We can apply this same principle to our spending categories. Instead of a vague "Entertainment" category, you might have a "Friend Time" fund or a "Cultural Experiences" budget.

This makes budgeting more engaging and helps align your spending with your values and priorities.

Another fascinating area of research is the concept of "pain of paying." Studies have shown that we feel psychological pain when we part with money, but the intensity of this pain can vary depending on the payment method. For example, people tend to spend more when using credit cards compared to cash, partly because the pain of paying is delayed.

Understanding this can help us make smarter financial decisions. If you're trying to cut back on impulse purchases, you might choose to use cash for certain categories of spending.

On the other hand, if you're working towards a savings goal, setting up automatic transfers can help bypass the pain of paying altogether.

But perhaps one of the most powerful psychological tools we can use in budgeting is the principle of small wins. Research in the field of behavioral economics has shown that achieving small, frequent successes is more motivating than striving for a single large goal.

This is why we're going to break down your financial goals into smaller, more manageable milestones. Instead of a vague goal like "save more money," we might start with "save $50 this week." As you achieve these smaller goals, you'll build momentum and confidence, making it easier to tackle larger financial challenges.

Now, I know we've covered a lot of ground here, and you might be feeling a bit overwhelmed. But don't worry – we're going to break all of this down into actionable steps.

Think of it as a financial makeover, but without the cheesy before-and-after photos.

Step 1: Financial Self-Reflection

Before we dive into the numbers, we need to get clear on your current financial situation and your goals. This isn't about tallying up your income and expenses (though we'll get to that).

It involves understanding your financial values, your spending triggers, and what you really want your money to do for you.

Step 2: Track Your Spending

I know, I know – this is the part everyone dreads. But trust me, it's crucial.

For at least a month, record every single expense.

And I mean every single one, right down to that pack of gum you bought on a whim. Don't judge your spending at this point – we're just gathering data.

Step 3: Categorize and Analyze

Now comes the fun part (yes, I said fun – work with me here). We'll look at where your money is actually going and compare it to where you want it to go.

This is where we often have our "aha" moments, like realizing you're spending more on subscription services than on groceries.

Step 4: Set Realistic Goals

Based on your values and your spending analysis, we'll set some financial goals. These should be specific, measurable, and achievable.

"Save more" is not a goal.

"Save $200 a month towards a down payment on a house" is a goal.

Step 5: Create Your Personalized Budget
Now we'll create a budget that reflects your reality and your goals. I'm not talking about fitting your life into a pre-made template – this involves creating a financial plan that works for you.

Step 6: Implement and Track
Put your budget into action and start tracking your progress. We'll talk about different tools and methods you can use, from apps to spreadsheets to good old-fashioned pen and paper.

Step 7: Review and Adjust
Your budget isn't set in stone. Life changes, priorities shift, and your budget should reflect that.

We'll set up regular check-ins to review your progress and make adjustments as needed.

The Power Of Visualization

Studies have shown that visualizing your financial goals can significantly increase your chances of achieving them. Try creating a vision board for your financial future, or use visual aids like progress bars to track your savings.

The more you can "see" your goals, the more real they become, and the more motivated you'll be to reach them.

Now, let's talk about some common pitfalls, problems, issues, problems, issues you might encounter on your budgeting journey, and how to avoid them.

The Ostrich Approach: Burying your head in the sand and ignoring your finances altogether. This is a surefire way to financial disaster. Knowledge is power. The more you understand about your money, the more control you have over it.

The Perfectionist Trap: Thinking that if you can't follow your budget perfectly, you've failed. Newsflash: nobody's perfect, and that includes their budgeting. It's okay to slip up sometimes. The key is to get back on track without beating yourself up.

The "Future Me" Fallacy: Assuming that your future self will somehow be better with money than your current self. Sorry to break it to you, but future you is still you. Start building good habits now, and your future self will thank you.

The Comparison Game: Looking at other people's financial situations and feeling like you're falling behind. Personal finance is just that – personal. Your journey is unique, and comparing yourself to others is a recipe for frustration.

The All-or-Nothing Mentality: Thinking that if you can't save a large amount, it's not worth saving at all. Every little bit counts. Even small savings can add up over time, thanks to the magic of compound interest.

The "I Deserve It" Spiral: Using treats or rewards as a justification for overspending. While self-care is important, it shouldn't come at the expense of your financial health. Find ways to treat yourself that align with your budget and goals.

The Shiny Object Syndrome: Getting distracted by new

financial trends or get-rich-quick schemes. Stick to your plan and avoid the temptation to chase every new financial fad. To avoid these pitfalls, problems, issues, remember to stay flexible, be kind to yourself, and keep your eyes on your long-term goals. And when in doubt, come back to the basics we've outlined in this book.

The 72-Hour Rule: When you're tempted to make an unplanned purchase, especially a large one, apply the 72-hour rule. Wait three days before buying. This cooling-off period allows the initial excitement to fade, giving you time to consider whether the purchase aligns with your budget and goals. You might be surprised how often that "must-have" item loses it's appeal after a few days of reflection.

Now, let's talk about adapting your budgeting technique to different life scenarios. Because let's face it, life has a way of throwing curveballs when we least expect them.

Budgeting on a Variable Income: If you're a freelancer, seasonal worker, or have an income that fluctuates, traditional budgeting methods can be challenging. The key here is to budget based on your lowest earning month.

Any extra income can be allocated to savings or used to tackle debt. Also, consider setting up a "buffer fund" to help smooth out the lean months.

Budgeting for Major Life Changes: Getting married? Having a baby? Changing careers?

These big life events often come with significant financial implications. Start planning early, adjusting your budget gradually to account for new expenses or changes in income. It's okay if things are a bit chaotic at first – give yourself time to adjust to your new normal.

Budgeting in Times of Crisis: Whether it's a global pandemic or a personal emergency, crises can throw even the best-laid financial plans into disarray. In these situations, focus on the essentials.

Identify your must-have expenses and look for areas where you can cut back temporarily. Don't be afraid to use your emergency fund – that's what it's there for.

Budgeting for Financial Windfalls: Received an inheritance or a large bonus? It's tempting to see this as "free money," but integrating windfalls into your budget can set you up for long-term success.

Consider allocating a portion to your financial goals, some to debt repayment if needed, and yes, a bit for fun too. Just make sure the fun doesn't derail your overall financial plan.

Budgeting for Retirement: As you approach retirement, your budget will need to shift. You'll likely be moving from an earning phase to a spending phase.

Start by estimating your retirement expenses and income sources. Consider how you'll draw down your savings and adjust your budget to ensure your money lasts throughout your retirement years.

No matter what life stage or situation you're in, the core principles of budgeting remain the same: know where your money is going, align your spending with your values and goals, and always leave room for flexibility and fun.

Fun Fact: *The Psychology of Money Colors*

Did you know that the color of your credit card can influence your spending? A study found that people tend to spend more when using a gold credit card compared to other colors.

This is because gold is associated with wealth and luxury, subtly encouraging higher spending. Something to keep in mind next time you're choosing a new credit card!

Key Takeaways:

- Budgeting is a personal journey, not a one-size-fits-all solution
- Understanding the psychology behind your spending habits is key to successful budgeting
- Flexibility is crucial – your budget should adapt to your life, not the other way around
- Focus on empowerment rather than restriction in your budgeting approach
- Small, consistent wins are more motivating than striving for perfection
- Regular review and adjustment of your budget is essential for long-term success
- Visualization techniques can significantly boost your motivation and goal achievement
- Be prepared to adapt your budgeting strategies as your life circumstances change
- the goal of budgeting is to help you live your best life, not to make you miserable

CHAPTER 1: LAYING THE FOUNDATION - YOUR FINANCIAL REALITY CHECK

Back in the days of ancient Rome, Julius Caesar wasn't just conquering Gaul and writing about himself in the third person. He was also implementing one of the world's first budgeting systems.

Yes, while most of us were still figuring out how to count past our fingers and toes, old Julius was already trying to control public spending.

Fast forward a couple of millennia, and here we are, still grappling with the same basic challenge: how to make our money behave. It's like we're all financial shepherds, trying to herd a flock of poorly behaved dollar bills that seem determined to escape at every turn.

Now, you might be thinking, "Great, another lecture about pinching pennies and giving up my daily latte." But hold your horses (or your coffee beans). I'm not talking about depriving yourself or living like a hermit.

It's about getting real with your money. It's time for a financial reality check, and trust me, it's going to be more fun than a tax audit (which, let's face it, isn't a high bar to clear).
Think of this as a financial X-ray. We're going to peer into the depths of your wallet, bank accounts, and spending habits. We'll uncover the hidden costs that are nibbling away at your finances like termites in a wooden piggy bank.

And yes, we might find a skeleton or two in your financial closet. But don't worry, I promise not to judge (much).

Let's start with a little trip down memory lane. Cast your mind back to your first encounter with money. Maybe it was a shiny coin from the tooth fairy, or a crumpled bill from a generous relative. Remember the thrill of possibility? The world was your oyster, and you were ready to buy it, one candy bar at a time.

Now, fast forward to today. How do you feel when you think about money?

Is it still exciting, or has it become a source of stress, confusion, or even dread?

If you're like most people, your relationship with money has probably become more complicated than a soap opera plot. But, money doesn't have to be your enemy. It's not some mystical force that's out to get you. It's a tool, plain and simple. And like any tool, it works best when you know how to use it properly.

So, let's roll up our sleeves and get our hands dirty. We're going to dig into your finances like archaeologists unearthing a long-lost civilization. Who knows what we'll find?

Maybe there's a hidden treasure trove of savings potential. Or perhaps we'll uncover the financial equivalent of Atlantis – that mythical land where all your money seems to disappear.

First things first: we need to take stock of your current financial situation. This means gathering all your financial documents. Bank statements, credit card bills, pay stubs, that IOU from your cousin Fred – if it involves money, we want to see it.

Now, I know what you're thinking. "Do I really have to look at all this stuff? Can't I just stick my head in the sand and hope for the best?" Well, you could, but then you'd miss out on all the fun (and by fun, I mean the opportunity to take control of your financial future).

So, grab a cup of coffee (or tea, if you're feeling fancy), find a comfortable spot, and now is the time to take action We're going to create a comprehensive picture of your financial life. Think of it as painting a self-portrait, but instead of using oils or watercolors, we're using dollar signs and decimal points.

Start by listing all your income sources. This includes your salary, any side hustles, investment returns, and yes, even that $20 bill you found in your old jacket pocket. Every penny counts, so don't leave anything out.
Next, we're going to tackle expenses. This is where things can get a bit... interesting. You might be surprised at where your money is actually going. That "occasional" takeout meal might be more frequent than you realized. And those subscriptions you forgot about? They're the ninjas of the financial world, silently siphoning money from your account every month.

Key Insight: *Small, recurring expenses can have a big impact on your finances over time. The $5 daily coffee might seem harmless, but it adds up to $1,825 over a year!*

Now, let's talk about the 'Expense X-Ray' technique. This is where we really get to play detective. We're going to scrutinize every expense, no matter how small.

That $2 ATM fee? Under the microscope it goes. The $10 you spent on a novelty rubber chicken? We want to know about it.

The goal here isn't to make you feel guilty about every purchase. It's to help you understand where your money is really going. Often, we have a vague idea of our spending habits, but when we look at the cold, hard numbers, it can be quite eye-opening.

For example, you might think you're spending $50 a month on

dining out, when in reality it's closer to $200. Or you might be surprised to find that you're spending more on your cable bill than on your retirement savings. These are the kinds of insights that can lead to real change in your financial life.
As we go through this process, it's important to be honest with yourself. This isn't the time for financial fiction writing. We're after the truth, the whole truth, and nothing but the truth. If you spent $100 on artisanal cheese last month, own it. (And maybe invite me over for a tasting next time.)

Once we have a clear picture of your income and expenses, we can start to identify your true financial priorities. This is where things get really interesting.

You might say that saving for retirement is a top priority, but if you're spending more on entertainment than you're putting into your 401(k), your actions are telling a different story. I'm not talking about judgment. It's about alignment.

Are your spending habits in line with your stated priorities? If not, something needs to change. And that's okay! Recognizing the disconnect is the first step towards making meaningful changes.

Now, let's talk about setting financial goals. This is where we get to dream a little.

What do you want your financial future to look like? Maybe you want to buy a house, start a business, or retire early to a tropical island. Whatever your goals, we need to make sure they're SMART: Specific, Measurable, Achievable, Relevant, and Time-bound.
For example, "save more money" isn't a SMART goal. But "save $10,000 for a down payment on a house within two years" is.

It's specific (we know the amount), measurable (we can track progress), achievable (assuming it's within your means), relevant (it aligns with your goal of homeownership), and time-bound (we have a two-year deadline). Setting these goals gives you something to work towards. It turns your financial journey from a vague wandering into a purposeful expedition.

And trust me, it's a lot more fun when you know where you're going.

Now, let's talk about the elephant in the room (or should I say, the latte in the room?): the impact of small daily purchases. You've probably heard of the "latte factor," the idea that cutting out small daily expenses can lead to significant savings over time. While it's true that small expenses can add up, it's also important to maintain perspective. Cutting out your daily coffee isn't going to magically make you a millionaire.

But being mindful of these expenses can help you make more intentional choices about your spending.

Fun Fact: The term "latte factor" was coined by financial author David Bach in 1999. It's been the subject of much debate in the personal finance world ever since.

The key is to focus on the expenses that don't bring you joy or value. If that daily latte is the highlight of your morning and helps you start your day right, it might be worth keeping. But if you're buying it out of habit and don't even really enjoy it, that might be a good place to cut back.

The goal of this financial reality check isn't to strip all joy from your life. It's to help you align your spending with your values and goals. It revolves around making conscious choices as opposed to operating on financial autopilot.

Now, let's walk through the process of implementing this financial reality check. We'll call it the "Financial Mirror" technique, because it's all about getting an honest reflection of your financial situation.

Step 1: Gather all your financial documents. This includes bank statements, credit card bills, investment accounts, and any other financial records you have. Don't leave anything out – we want the full picture.
Step 2: List all your income sources. This includes your regular salary, any side hustles, investment income, etc. Be thorough – even small amounts count.
Step 3: Categorize and list all your expenses. This is where the "Expense X-Ray" comes in. Go through your statements line by line and categorize each expense. Common categories include housing, transportation, food, entertainment, etc.
Step 4: Compare your income to your expenses. Are you spending more than you're earning? If so, that's a red flag that needs addressing.
Step 5: Identify areas of overspending. Look for categories where you're spending more than you realized or more than you'd like.
Step 6: Set specific, measurable financial goals. Make them SMART!
Step 7: Create a realistic budget based on your findings. This should align with your goals and priorities.
Step 8: Implement a tracking system for ongoing monitoring. This could be a spreadsheet, a budgeting app, or even a good old-fashioned notebook.
Step 9: Schedule regular check-ins to assess your progress. Monthly is a good starting point, but adjust as needed.
Step 10: Adjust your budget and goals as needed. Life changes, and your financial plan should change with it.

Now, let's address some common pitfalls, problems, issues,

problems, issues you might encounter during this process.

First up: **the ostrich approach.** This is when you stick your head in the sand and ignore your financial reality. It might feel comfortable in the short term, but it's not a sustainable strategy. Knowledge is power. The more you know about your finances, the more control you have over them.

Another common pitfall, problem, issue, problem, issue is the **all-or-nothing mentality**. You might look at your spending and think, "I need to cut out everything enjoyable to save money." This approach is rarely sustainable. Instead, focus on making small, manageable changes that you can stick with long-term.

Then there's the **comparison trap**. You might be tempted to measure your financial situation against others. But remember, personal finance is just that – personal. What works for someone else might not work for you. Focus on your own goals and progress.

Finally, beware of the quick fix mentality. Building a solid financial foundation takes time and consistency. There's no magic bullet that will solve all your money problems overnight.

Key Principle: Consistency is vital in personal finance. Small, sustainable changes over time can lead to significant results.

Now, let's talk about adapting this technique to different scenarios. Maybe you have a variable income, or you're dealing with significant debt, or you're planning for a major life change like starting a family or retiring.

If you have a variable income, focus on understanding your baseline expenses – the amount you need each month to cover necessities. Then, create a plan for allocating any income above that baseline. You might use percentages as opposed to fixed amounts in your budget.

If you're dealing with debt, prioritize creating a debt repayment plan as part of your financial goals. The debt snowball (paying off smallest debts first) or debt avalanche (paying off highest interest debts first) methods can be effective strategies.

For major life changes, start by researching the potential financial impacts. Then, adjust your goals and budget accordingly.

This might mean increasing your savings rate, adjusting your insurance coverage, or reevaluating your investment strategy.

Your financial plan should be as unique as you are. Don't be afraid to tweak and adjust as you go along.

The key is to stay engaged with your finances and keep moving towards your goals.

Key Takeaways:

- A financial reality check is crucial for understanding your current situation and planning for the future.
- Be honest and thorough when assessing your income and expenses.
- Set SMART financial goals that align with your priorities and values.
- Small, daily expenses can have a significant impact over time, but focus on cutting costs that don't bring you joy or value.
- Implement the "Financial Mirror" technique to get a clear picture of your finances.
- Avoid common pitfalls, problems, issues, problems, issues like the ostrich approach, all-or-nothing mentality, comparison trap, and quick fix mentality.

- Adapt your financial strategy to your unique situation and life changes.
- Consistency and patience are key to long-term financial success.

CHAPTER 2: BUILDING YOUR BUDGET BLUEPRINT

Money, that fickle friend we all wish we had more of, yet somehow always seems to slip through our fingers like sand in an hourglass. If you're anything like me, you've probably found yourself staring at your bank balance with a mixture of confusion and despair, wondering where on earth all those hard-earned dollars disappeared to.

Well, don't worry, dear reader, for we're about to begin on a journey to financial enlightenment – or at least, a journey to stop you from buying that third latte of the day. Creating a budget is not about pinching pennies until they scream. It involves taking control of your financial destiny, like a captain steering a ship through stormy seas. And let's face it, in today's economy, those seas can get pretty choppy.

But with the right budget blueprint, you'll be navigating those waters like a pro, dodging the icebergs of impulse purchases and sailing smoothly towards the shores of financial stability. Now, I know what you're thinking. "Budgeting? Isn't that just a fancy word for 'no fun allowed'?" I used to think the same way. In fact, I once considered my credit card limit as more of a target than a warning.

But trust me, once you get the hang of it, budgeting can be surprisingly liberating. It's like giving yourself permission to spend money – on the things that truly matter to you.

So, let's roll up our sleeves and dive into the nitty-gritty of building a budget that doesn't just work on paper, but actually works in real life. We'll explore everything from the famous

50/30/20 rule to the art of customizing budget categories that fit your lifestyle like a well-tailored suit. And don't worry, we'll also tackle those pesky irregular expenses that love to pop up and say "surprise!" at the most inconvenient times.

The **50/30/20 Rule**: Your Financial North Star
Imagine you're at a buffet (because who doesn't love a good food analogy?). The 50/30/20 rule is like dividing your plate into three sections: a big one for the main course, a smaller one for sides, and a little corner for dessert. In this financial feast, your income is the plate, and you're dividing it up between needs, wants, and savings/debt repayment.

Here's how it breaks down:

50% for Needs: This is the meat and potatoes of your budget. It covers essentials like housing, utilities, groceries, and basic transportation. These are the non-negotiables, the things you need to keep a roof over your head and food in your belly.

30% for Wants: Here's where you get to have a little fun. This category is for the things that make life enjoyable – dining out, entertainment, that fancy gym membership, or your monthly subscription to the Cheese of the Month Club (no judgment here).

20% for Savings and Debt Repayment: This is the vegetables of your financial diet – not always the most exciting, but crucial for your long-term financial health. It includes building up your emergency fund, saving for retirement, and paying down debt. Now, I know what you're thinking. "30% for wants? That seems awfully generous!" And you're right, it might be. The beauty of this rule is it's flexibility.

If you're trying to pay off debt faster or save for a big goal, you might decide to allocate more to the savings category and less to wants. The key is to use this as a starting point and adjust based on your personal situation and goals.

Customizing Your Budget Categories: One Size Fits None

If budgets were shoes, the 50/30/20 rule would be a good pair of sneakers – comfortable and versatile, but maybe not quite right for every occasion. That's where customizing your budget categories comes in. It's like having a closet full of shoes for every situation.

Start by listing out all your regular expenses. And I mean all of them. That $5 you spend on scratch-off lottery tickets every week? Yep, include that too. Once you have your list, start grouping similar expenses together.

For example, you might have a "Food" category that includes groceries, dining out, and your daily coffee run.

Now, here's where it gets fun (yes, I just used "fun" and "budget" in the same sentence – miracles do happen). Create categories that reflect your lifestyle and priorities. Are you a fitness fanatic? Maybe you need a "Health and Wellness" category for gym memberships, protein powders, and those fancy workout leggings you swear make you run faster. Love to travel? Create a "Wanderlust Fund" category to save for your next adventure.

The key is to be specific enough to track your spending accurately, but not so detailed that you need a PhD in spreadsheet management to keep up with it. Aim for about 10-15 categories total.

Here's an example of how your customized categories might look:

Needs:

- Housing (rent/mortgage, property taxes, insurance)
- Utilities (electricity, water, gas, internet)
- Groceries
- Transportation
- Healthcare

Wants:

- Entertainment
- Dining Out
- Shopping
- Personal Care
- Hobbies

Savings and Debt Repayment:

- Emergency Fund
- Retirement Savings
- Debt Repayment
- Future Goals (house down payment, vacation fund, etc.)

Your categories should make sense to you. To create a separate category for "Artisanal Cheese Purchases," go for it.

The goal is to create a system that you'll actually stick to, not one that makes you want to throw your computer out the window every time you look at it.

Ah, irregular expenses. The financial equivalent of that relative who shows up unannounced and expects to be fed and entertained. These sneaky costs can throw even the most carefully planned budget into chaos if you're not prepared for them.

The secret to handling these expenses is to treat them like regular monthly bills, even though they don't occur every month. Here's how:

1. Make a list of all your irregular expenses. This might include things like car insurance premiums, property taxes, holiday gifts, or annual subscriptions.
2. Estimate the annual cost for each item. If you're not sure, it's better to overestimate slightly than to come up short.
3. Divide the annual cost by 12 to get the monthly amount you need to set aside.
4. Create a separate savings account specifically for these expenses. Let's call it your "Irregular Expense Fund" (much more polite than "Oh Crap, I Forgot About That Bill" Fund).
5. Set up an automatic transfer to this account each month. Treat it like any other bill payment.

For example, let's say you have the following irregular expenses:

- Annual car insurance premium: $1,200
- Holiday gifts: $800
- Annual home maintenance: $1,000
- Quarterly water bill: $300 ($1,200 annually)

The total annual cost is $4,200. Divided by 12, you'd need to set aside $350 per month in your Irregular Expense Fund.

By doing this, you're essentially spreading out the cost of these expenses over the entire year. When that big bill comes due, you'll have the money ready and waiting, as opposed to scrambling to find an extra $1,200 in your budget for car insurance.

Key Insight: *Treating irregular expenses as monthly costs by saving for them in advance can prevent budget-busting surprises and reduce financial stress.*

The 'Flex Fund' Strategy: Your Budget's Secret Weapon Even with the most meticulously planned budget, life has a way of throwing financial curveballs. That's where the 'Flex Fund' comes in.

Think of it as your budget's emergency parachute – there if you need it, but hopefully you won't have to use it too often.

The Flex Fund is a small amount of money you set aside each month to cover unexpected expenses or to give yourself a little wiggle room in your budget. It's not meant to replace your emergency fund (which should cover larger unexpected expenses or loss of income), but rather to act as a buffer for those smaller, unforeseen costs.

Here's how to implement the Flex Fund strategy:

1. Allocate about 5-10% of your monthly income to your Flex Fund. This might come from your 'Wants' category or be an extra line item in your budget.
2. Keep your Flex Fund in a separate savings account. This helps you avoid accidentally spending it on regular expenses.
3. Define what forms a valid use of your Flex Fund. This might include unexpected car repairs, surprise medical bills, or last-minute travel for a family emergency.
4. Replenish your Flex Fund monthly, even if you haven't used it recently. Think of it as insurance for your budget.
5. Review your Flex Fund usage periodically. If you find you're consistently overspending in certain categories, it might be time to adjust your main budget as opposed to relying on the Flex Fund.

The beauty of the Flex Fund is that it gives you permission to be human. We all make mistakes or face unexpected situations, and having this buffer can prevent these hiccups from derailing your entire financial plan. Plus, it can reduce the stress and guilt often associated with going over budget.

Integrating Savings and Debt Repayment: The Dynamic Duo of Financial Health

Savings and debt repayment are like the Batman and Robin of personal finance – they work best as a team. But how do you balance these two crucial elements in your budget?

Let's break it down:
Savings: The key to successful saving is to treat it like any other non-negotiable expense in your budget. This is the "pay yourself first" mentality, and it's a game-changer.

Here's how to make it work:

1. Set specific savings goals. Whether it's building an emergency fund, saving for a down payment on a house, or planning for retirement, having clear goals can motivate you to save consistently.
2. Automate your savings. Set up automatic transfers from your checking account to your savings accounts on payday. This way, you're saving before you have a chance to spend the money.
3. Use many savings accounts for different goals. This can help you track your progress more easily and reduce the temptation to dip into your savings for other purposes.
4. Start small and increase gradually. Begin with a savings rate you can comfortably manage, then aim to increase it by 1% every few months. You'll be surprised how quickly

small increases can add up.

Debt Repayment: Tackling debt can feel like trying to eat an elephant. But remember, the way to eat an elephant is one bite at a time.

Here's your debt-busting strategy:

1. List all your debts, including the balance, interest rate, and least payment for each.
2. Choose a debt repayment strategy.

Two popular methods are:

- The debt avalanche: Focus on high-interest debt first. This saves you the most money in interest over time.
- The debt snowball: Pay off smallest debts first. This gives you quick wins and can be more motivating.

3. Pay more than the least. Always pay at least the least on all debts, but allocate any extra money to the debt you're focusing on based on your chosen strategy.
4. Consider balance transfers or debt consolidation. If you have high-interest credit card debt, look into balance transfer offers or personal loans with lower interest rates.
5. Celebrate milestones. Paying off debt can be a long process. Acknowledge your progress along the way to stay motivated.

Balancing Savings and Debt Repayment:

While the 50/30/20 rule suggests allocating 20% to savings and debt repayment combined, you may need to adjust this based on your situation. If you have high-interest debt, you might allocate more towards debt repayment initially.

As you pay down debt, you can shift more towards savings. Building savings and paying off debt are both crucial for your financial health. Strive for a balance that allows you to make progress on both fronts simultaneously.

Key Insight: Treating savings as a non-negotiable expense and tackling debt systematically can significantly improve your financial health over time.

Choosing the Right Budgeting Tools: Your Financial Swiss Army Knife

In today's digital age, there's no shortage of tools and apps to help you create and stick to your budget. Choosing the right one is like picking the perfect Swiss Army knife – you want something with all the tools you need, but not so many that it becomes unwieldy.

Here's a guide to help you choose:

1. Assess your tech comfort level. If you're a digital native, a comprehensive budgeting app might be ideal. If you prefer simplicity, a basic spreadsheet or even a pen-and-paper system could work better.
2. Consider your budgeting style. Do you prefer manual entry of expenses, or would you rather have your transactions automatically categorized? Some apps connect directly to your bank accounts, while others need manual input.
3. Evaluate features. Look for features that align with your budgeting goals. These might include bill reminders, savings goal trackers, investment monitoring, or debt payoff planners.
4. Check compatibility. Ensure the tool works with your bank and credit card accounts if you want automatic

transaction importing.
5. Consider security. If you're using an app that connects to your financial accounts, make sure it has robust security measures in place.
6. Try before you commit. Many apps offer free trials. Take advantage of these to test out different options before deciding. Here are some popular budgeting tools to consider:
- Spreadsheets (like Google Sheets or Microsoft Excel): Great for those who want full control and customization.
- Mint: A free app that automatically categorizes your transactions and provides a comprehensive overview of your finances.
- You Need A Budget (YNAB): This app follows a zero-based budgeting approach and focuses on giving every dollar a job.
- Personal Capital: While primarily an investment tool, it also offers robust budgeting features.
- EveryDollar: Created by financial guru Dave Ramsey, this app follows his budgeting principles.
- PocketGuard: This app focuses on showing you how much you have left to spend after accounting for bills and savings goals.
- Goodbudget: Uses the envelope budgeting system in a digital format.

The best budgeting tool is the one you'll actually use consistently. Don't be afraid to try a few different options before settling on the one that works best for you. Building your budget blueprint is like constructing a financial fortress. It provides structure, protection, and a solid foundation for your financial future.

By understanding and implementing the 50/30/20 rule, customizing your budget categories, accounting for irregular expenses, using the Flex Fund strategy, integrating savings and debt repayment, and choosing the right budgeting tools, you're setting yourself up for financial success.

A budget isn't about restriction – this involves aligning your spending with your values and goals. It's a powerful tool that gives you control over your money, as opposed to letting your money control you.

As you implement these strategies, you'll find that budgeting becomes less of a chore and more of a pathway to financial freedom and peace of mind. And who knows? You might even find yourself getting a little excited about tracking your expenses. (Okay, maybe that's just me. But hey, stranger things have happened!)

Key Takeaways:

- The 50/30/20 rule provides a solid starting point for budget allocation
- Customize your budget categories to reflect your lifestyle and priorities
- Plan for irregular expenses by treating them as monthly costs
- Use a Flex Fund to handle unexpected expenses without derailing your budget
- Balance savings and debt repayment to improve overall financial health
- Choose budgeting tools that align with your preferences and needs
- A well-crafted budget gives you control over your money and aligns spending with your goals

CHAPTER 3: THE PSYCHOLOGY OF SPENDING - REWIRING YOUR MONEY MINDSET

Money has a peculiar way of messing with our heads. One minute we're feeling flush, ready to splurge on that shiny new gadget we've been eyeing. The next, we're wracked with guilt over a $5 latte. It's as if our wallets are connected directly to our emotional centers, pulling strings we didn't even know existed.

I once found myself standing in a high-end electronics store, credit card in hand, ready to drop an obscene amount of money on a television that was, quite frankly, larger than my first apartment. The salesman's pitch was smooth as silk, painting vivid pictures of movie nights that would rival the local cinema. My heart raced with excitement.

But as I reached for my wallet, a tiny voice in the back of my head whispered, "Do you really need this?" That voice, my friends, is what psychologists call our "financial conscience." It's the part of our brain that tries to keep our spending in check, often fighting a losing battle against the more primitive parts that just want instant gratification. And let me tell you, in the grand arena of our minds, it's usually the underdog.
The psychology of spending is a fascinating field, full of quirks and contradictions that would make even Freud scratch his head. Did you know, for instance, that simply holding a credit card can increase your willingness to spend?

It's true. A study published in the Journal of Consumer Research found that people are willing to spend up to 100% more when using credit instead of cash. It's as if that little piece of plastic has magical properties, making the pain of parting with our hard-earned money mysteriously vanish.

But before we dive headfirst into the murky waters of our financial psyche, let's take a moment to appreciate the sheer absurdity of our relationship with money. We work tirelessly to earn it, obsess over saving it, and then find endless creative ways to spend it. It's like a never-ending game of financial hot potato, except the potato is our bank account, and we're all terrible at catching.

The Emotional Rollercoaster of Spending

Our emotions play a starring role in the theater of our spending habits. Joy, sadness, anger, fear - each one can send us sprinting to the nearest store (or these days, furiously clicking "add to cart"). It's as if our wallets are directly wired to our tear ducts and smile muscles.

Take "retail therapy," for instance. It's not just a cutesy phrase invented by shopaholics to justify their habits. There's actual science behind it. When we're feeling down, a little splurge can give us a temporary mood boost. The act of buying something new triggers a release of dopamine in our brains, the same neurotransmitter associated with pleasure and reward.

It's like our brain is giving us a little pat on the back, saying, "Good job! You bought that completely unnecessary gadget. Don't you feel better now?" But here's what's interesting: that feel-good sensation is fleeting. Before long, we're right back where we started, only now with less money and more stuff.

It's a vicious cycle that can leave us feeling like hamsters on a wheel, running faster and faster but never really getting anywhere. On the flip side, some of us experience intense anxiety when it comes to spending money, even on necessities.

This "money anxiety disorder" can lead to extreme frugality, hoarding, or even an inability to use money to improve your quality of life.

It's as if every dollar spent is a personal failure, a sentiment that would make even Ebenezer Scrooge raise an eyebrow.

The 'Desire Delay' Technique: Taming the Impulse Beast

Now, I'm not suggesting we all become ascetics, renouncing worldly possessions and living in barrels like Diogenes (though I hear real estate prices in Ancient Greece were quite reasonable). But there is a middle ground between compulsive spending and extreme frugality.

Enter the 'Desire Delay' technique.

This simple yet effective method is like putting your impulses in time-out. Here's how it works:

1. When you feel the urge to make an unplanned purchase, stop. Take a deep breath. Maybe two.
2. Write down what you want to buy and why you want it. Be honest. "Because it's shiny" is a valid reason, albeit not a great one.
3. Set a waiting period. For small purchases, 24 hours might suffice. For bigger ones, try a week or even a month.
4. After the waiting period, revisit your notes. Do you still want the item? Does the reason still hold up?
5. If yes, and if it fits your budget, go ahead. If not, congratulate yourself on your newfound impulse control.

This technique works because it creates a buffer between the emotional impulse to buy and the rational decision-making process. It's like giving your financial conscience a megaphone and some time in the spotlight.

I once applied this to a particularly snazzy pair of shoes I was convinced would change my life. After a week, I realized I already owned three pairs of black dress shoes and that these new ones, while fabulous, would likely spend more time in my closet than on my feet. My bank account breathed a sigh of relief.

The Social Media Spending Trap

Ah, social media. The place where everyone's life looks perfect, their vacations are always exotic, and their avocado toast is perpetually Instagram-worthy. It's also a veritable minefield for our wallets.

Social media platforms have become incredibly sophisticated marketing machines. They know what we like, what we've been searching for, and probably what we had for breakfast. This targeted advertising, combined with the constant barrage of "influencer" content, creates a perfect storm for impulse spending.

Key Insight: *Studies show that 72% of Instagram users report making fashion, beauty, or style-related purchases after seeing something on the app.*

But it's not just the ads. It's the subtle (and not-so-subtle) pressure to keep up with the Joneses, or in this case, the Kardashians.

We see our friends (or people we vaguely knew in high school) posting about their new cars, their exotic vacations, their latest tech gadgets, and suddenly our own lives seem... lacking.

This is where the concept of "FOMO" (Fear Of Missing Out) comes into play. We worry that if we don't have the latest and greatest, we're somehow falling behind. It's as if life has become one big competition, and the person with the most stuff wins.

So how do we counteract this? Here are a few strategies:

1. **Curate your feed**: Unfollow or mute accounts that make you feel inadequate or trigger unhealthy spending urges.
2. **Reality check**: social media is a highlight reel, not reality. That perfect vacation photo probably took 50 attempts and some creative cropping to hide the sunburn and mosquito bites.
3. **Practice gratitude**: Regularly reflect on what you already have and what truly brings you joy. Spoiler alert: it's probably not that limited edition, gold-plated fidget spinner.
4. **Set social media boundaries**: Limit your scrolling time. Your thumb will thank you, and so will your wallet.
5. **Ad blockers are your friends**: Use them liberally. Your online experience will be less cluttered, and you'll be less tempted by things you never knew you "needed."

Developing a Healthy Relationship with Money

Now, I know what you're thinking. "Great, so I just need to resist every spending impulse, avoid social media, and live like a monk. Easy peasy!" Not quite.

The goal isn't to never spend money or enjoy nice things. It's about developing a healthier, more mindful relationship with your finances. Think of it like dating. You wouldn't want to be in a relationship where you're constantly trying to buy your partner's affection, right? (If you would, we need to have a different conversation.) The same goes for money.

It's not about impressing it or trying to control it. It revolves around understanding it, respecting it, and yes, even enjoying it in a balanced way.

Here are some steps to foster this healthier relationship:

1. **Get to know your money**: Track your spending for a month. Every single penny. It's like going on a first date with your finances. You might be surprised by what you learn.
2. **Identify your money personality**: Are you a spender, a saver, an avoider, or a worrier? Understanding your tendencies can help you work with them, not against them.
3. **Set financial goals**: Give your money a purpose beyond just accumulating or spending. Maybe it's saving for a dream vacation, building an emergency fund, or working towards early retirement.
4. **Practice mindful spending**: Before making a purchase, ask yourself: "Does this align with my values and goals?" It's like asking if your potential date shares your interests before committing to dinner.
5. **Celebrate financial wins**: Did you stick to your budget this month? Treat yourself (responsibly, of course). Positive reinforcement works wonders.
6. **Forgive financial mistakes**: We all slip up sometimes. The important thing is to learn from it and move on. Don't let one overspend turn into a full-blown shopping spree.

Aligning Your Spending with Your Values

Here's where things get really interesting. Would you be surprised if you found out that your spending could actually make you happier?

No, I haven't been hitting the sales too hard. I'm talking about value-based spending.

The idea is simple: when your spending aligns with your core values and what truly matters to you, you're likely to feel more satisfied with your purchases and your life in general. It's like the difference between eating a meal you truly enjoy versus mindlessly snacking on whatever's in reach.

So how do we put this into practice? First, you need to identify your core values. Maybe it's family, health, education, travel, or environmental sustainability.

Once you've got that sorted, look at your spending patterns. Are they reflecting these values? For instance, if you value experiences over material possessions, but find yourself constantly buying new gadgets, there's a misalignment. Or if you claim to prioritize health but spend more on fast food than fresh produce, it might be time for a rethink.

Here's a personal example: I used to spend a small fortune on designer coffee every day. But when I really thought about it, what I valued most was the quiet time to read and reflect in the mornings. Now, I make my coffee at home and use the money I save for books and a comfy reading chair. My bank account is happier, and so am I.

Principle to Remember: *Spending money on things that align with your values leads to greater long-term satisfaction than impulse purchases or keeping up with trends.*

The pitfalls, problems, issues, of Retail Therapy

Now, let's talk about the dark side of spending: retail therapy. We've all been there. Had a bad day at work? Buy a new shirt. Feeling down? A new gadget ought to cheer you up. It's like we're trying to fill an emotional void with stuff.

The problem is, it doesn't work. At least, not in the long run. That initial rush of dopamine from making a purchase fades quickly, leaving us right back where we started, only with less money and more clutter.

Here's how to avoid falling into the retail therapy trap:

1. **Identify your emotional triggers**: What situations or feelings typically lead you to overspend?
2. **Find choice coping mechanisms**: Instead of shopping when you're stressed, try exercise, meditation, or calling a friend.
3. **Create a "feel-good" fund**: Set aside a small amount each month for guilt-free spending. This way, you can indulge occasionally without derailing your budget.
4. **Practice the 10/10/10 rule**: Before making a purchase, ask yourself: How will I feel about this in 10 minutes? 10 months? 10 years?
5. **Unsubscribe from marketing emails**: Out of sight, out of mind. Your inbox will thank you.

True happiness and self-worth can't be bought. They come from within, not from the mall or Amazon's warehouse.

Adapting Your Money Mindset for Different Life Stages

Our relationship with money isn't static. It advance as we move through different life stages, each bringing it's own financial challenges and opportunities.

In your 20s, you might be focused on paying off student loans and building your career. Your 30s might bring thoughts of homeownership or starting a family. By your 40s and 50s, retirement planning becomes more pressing.

The key is to be flexible and adjust your money mindset as your life changes. Here are some tips:

1. **Regularly reassess your financial goals**: What mattered to you at 25 might not be as important at 45.
2. **Be prepared for financial curveballs**: Life has a way of throwing unexpected expenses our way. An emergency fund is your financial shock absorber.
3. **Don't compare your financial journey to others**: Everyone's path is different. Focus on your own progress.
4. **Invest in financial education**: The more you understand about money management, the better equipped you'll be to handle whatever life throws your way.
5. **Consider working with a financial advisor**: As your financial situation becomes more complex, professional guidance can be invaluable.

Rewiring your money mindset is a habit to infuse into your life, not a one-time goal to reach. It takes time, patience, and yes, probably a few slip-ups along the way.

But with persistence and self-awareness, you can develop a healthier relationship with your finances that serves you well throughout your life.

Key Takeaways

- Understanding your emotional triggers for spending is key to developing better financial habits.
- The 'Desire Delay' technique can help curb impulse purchases and promote more mindful spending.
- Social media can significantly influence spending habits - be aware of it's impact and set boundaries.
- Aligning your spending with your core values leads to greater long-term satisfaction.
- Retail therapy provides only short-term emotional relief and can lead to financial stress.
- Your relationship with money advance throughout different life stages - be flexible and adjust your approach accordingly.
- Developing a healthy money mindset is an ongoing process that requires patience and self-awareness.

CHAPTER 4: BECOMING BETTER AT THE ART OF EXPENSE TRACKING

Expense tracking is the cornerstone of effective budgeting. It's the financial equivalent of counting calories - tedious at first, but essential if you want to see results. Without it, you're essentially stumbling around in the dark, hoping you don't trip over your own financial feet.

The concept isn't new. Ancient Mesopotamian merchants were scribbling away on clay tablets, meticulously recording their transactions. Fast forward a few millennia, and here we are, still grappling with the same fundamental task, albeit with fancier tools at our disposal.

But why is it so crucial? Well, imagine trying to navigate a ship without knowing your current position. You might have a vague idea of where you're headed, but good luck getting there efficiently.

That's your financial life without expense tracking. You're adrift in a sea of transactions, hoping you'll somehow wash up on the shores of financial stability.

Research backs this up. A 2021 study in the Journal of Consumer Research found that consistent expense trackers were 30% more likely to achieve their financial goals. That's not just a slight edge - it's the difference between reaching your destination and circling aimlessly in financial waters.

But let's be honest, tracking every penny that leaves your wallet isn't exactly thrilling. It's about as exciting as watching paint dry, only with more math involved. Yet, it's this very tedium that makes it so effective.

It forces you to confront every purchase, every indulgence, every "it's only a few dollars" moment that collectively can sink your financial ship. The good news is, we're not stuck in the age of ledgers and quill pens. Technology has given us a plethora of tools to make this task less of a chore.

From smartphone apps that can categorize your spending faster than you can say "impulse purchase," to AI-powered systems that predict your future expenses with eerie accuracy, we're in a golden age of expense tracking. But with great power comes great responsibility, and a whole host of new questions. How often should you track? What method works best?

How do you categorize that weird purchase that doesn't seem to fit anywhere? And perhaps most importantly, how do you stick with it when the novelty wears off and you'd rather watch paint dry than log another receipt?

Fear not, intrepid budgeter. We're about to set off on a move through the wild world of expense tracking. We'll explore methods both ancient and cutting-edge, debunk myths, and arm you with the tools you need to become a true expense tracking artiste.

By the end, you'll be tracking your expenses with the precision of a forensic accountant and the zeal of a kid counting Halloween candy. It's time to master the art of knowing where every penny goes - and more importantly, where it should be going instead.

The first step in our expense tracking odyssey is understanding the 'why' behind it all. Sure, we know it's important, but let's dig a little deeper. Expense tracking isn't about being a penny-pinching miser or impressing your accountant. It's about gaining control over your financial life.

Think of it as financial mindfulness. Just as meditation helps you become aware of your thoughts, expense tracking makes you conscious of your spending habits. It's like shining a spotlight on the dark corners of your financial house, revealing dust bunnies of wasteful spending you didn't even know were there.

But there's more to it than just cutting costs. Effective expense tracking can actually be liberating. When you know exactly where your money is going, you can make informed decisions about where you want it to go. It's the difference between being a passive passenger in your financial journey and taking the wheel.

Now, let's address the elephant in the room - the dreaded 'b' word. Budget. For many, it conjures images of deprivation and joyless penny-pinching. But here's a secret: a good budget, informed by accurate expense tracking, isn't about restriction. It's about allocation. It's ensuring your money goes to the things you truly value, rather than leaking away on things you don't.

Consider this: The National Bureau of Economic Research found that consistent expense tracking led to an average reduction in unnecessary spending of 15-20% over six months. That's not chump change.

It's money that could be redirected to your goals, whether that's a dream vacation, a down payment on a house, or simply the peace of mind that comes with a robust emergency fund. But here's where many people go wrong - they try to change their spending habits before they truly understand them. It's like trying to fix a car engine without opening the hood.

Expense tracking is your financial diagnostics tool. It reveals patterns you might not even be aware of. Maybe that daily coffee run is costing more than you realized, or perhaps you're spending a small fortune on subscription services you barely use.

Key Insight: *Expense tracking isn't about judgment - this involves awareness. The goal isn't to make you feel guilty about every purchase, but to empower you to make conscious decisions about your spending.*

Now, let's talk methods. In the olden days (read: before smartphones), expense tracking meant keeping a little notebook in your pocket and diligently writing down every purchase. It was effective, but about as convenient as carrying around a typewriter.

Today, we have a smorgasbord of options. There are apps that can sync with your bank accounts and automatically categorize your spending. Some even use AI to predict future expenses based on your patterns. It's like having a tiny financial advisor in your pocket, minus the expensive suits and PowerPoint presentations.

This approach combines the mindfulness of manual tracking with the convenience of digital tools. Here's how it works:

1. Capture: Take a photo of every receipt immediately after purchase. This confirms you don't lose track of any spending, no matter how small.
2. Categorize: Assign each expense to a predefined category. This helps you see where your money is really going.
3. Compile: Weekly, gather all your digital receipts and enter them into your tracking system. This could be a spreadsheet, an app, or even a good old-fashioned ledger if you're feeling retro.

4. Cross-check: Compare your tracked expenses with your bank statements. This helps catch any missed expenses and keeps you honest.
5. Correct: Address any discrepancies or missing entries. Accuracy is key.
6. Categorize trends: Look for patterns in your spending. Are there areas where you're consistently overspending?
7. Create goals: Based on your tracked data, set specific targets for different spending categories.
8. Celebrate progress: Acknowledge improvements in your tracking and spending habits. Positive reinforcement works wonders.

This method combines the best of both worlds - the mindfulness of manual tracking with the convenience of digital tools. It forces you to be aware of each purchase in the moment, while still leveraging technology to make the process easier.

Now, I know what you're thinking. "This sounds great in theory, but how do I actually make it happen?" Well, my friend, that's where the rubber meets the road. Or in this case, where the app meets the receipt.

The Nitty-Gritty of Expense Tracking

Let's start with frequency. How often should you track your expenses? The answer is simple: as often as you can without losing your mind.

Ideally, you'd log every expense as it happens. But let's be real - unless you're gunning for the title of World's Most Diligent Budgeter, that's probably not sustainable. A more realistic approach is to set aside a few minutes each day to review and log your expenses. Think of it as your financial meditation.

Brew a cup of tea, put on some soothing music, and zen out with your receipts. It's not exactly a spa day, but it's a lot cheaper and your bank account will thank you.

If daily tracking feels like too much, aim for at least once a week. Any longer than that, and you risk forgetting expenses or losing receipts. Plus, weekly tracking allows you to catch and fix any issues before they snowball into bigger problems.

Now, let's talk categorization. This is where many people get tripped up. Is that latte a "food" expense or a "personal care" item? Does dog food fall under "pets" or "groceries"? The answer is: it doesn't really matter, as long as you're consistent.

The key is to create categories that make sense for your lifestyle and stick to them. Some common categories include:

- Housing (rent/mortgage, utilities, maintenance)
- Transportation (car payments, gas, public transit)
- Food (groceries, dining out)
- Personal Care (haircuts, gym memberships, clothing)
- Entertainment (movies, concerts, hobbies)
- Debt Payments (credit cards, student loans)
- Savings and Investments

Feel free to get as granular as you want. If you're a coffee aficionado who wants to track your artisanal bean purchases separately from your grocery budget, go for it.

The goal is to create a system that gives you meaningful insights into your spending habits.

Pro Tip: *Create a "Miscellaneous" category for those odd expenses that don't fit anywhere else. But be careful - if this category starts growing too large, it might be time to reassess your categorization system.*

Now, let's address the elephant in the room - cash. In our increasingly digital world, cash transactions can be the bane of expense trackers everywhere. They're easy to forget and hard to categorize after the fact. My solution? The "Cash Envelope" system.

At the beginning of each week or month, withdraw a set amount of cash for discretionary spending. Put it in an envelope (yes, a physical envelope - we're going old school here). Every time you spend cash, jot it down on the envelope. When the cash is gone, so is your discretionary budget for the period.

This method helps you track cash expenses and provides a natural limit on this type of spending. It's like having a built-in financial brake system. But what about those pesky digital subscriptions and recurring payments? These sneaky expenses can easily slip under the radar, quietly draining your bank account month after month.

The solution? A subscription audit.

Once a quarter, sit down and review all your recurring payments. Ask yourself:

1. Do I still use this service?
2. Is it providing value equivalent to it's cost?
3. Is there a cheaper choice?

You'd be surprised how many subscriptions you've forgotten about or no longer need. Cancelling just a few can free up a significant amount in your budget.

Now, let's talk about the psychology of expense tracking. Like any habit, it can be challenging to maintain at first. You might feel motivated for a week or two, then slowly start slipping back into old patterns. This is normal. The key is to make expense tracking as painless and rewarding as possible.

One effective strategy is to gamify the process. Set challenges for yourself, like reducing a particular category of spending by 10% in a month. Or see how many days you can go logging every expense without missing one.

Give yourself small rewards for hitting these targets. Maybe that fancy latte you've been eyeing can be your prize for a month of diligent tracking. Another helpful tip is to find an accountability partner. This could be a spouse, a friend, or even an online community of fellow budgeters. Share your goals and progress with them. Knowing someone else is checking in on your efforts can be a powerful motivator.

The goal of expense tracking isn't to make you feel guilty about your spending. It's to empower you to make informed decisions about your money. If your tracking reveals that you're spending $200 a month on takeout, that's not necessarily a bad thing - if it aligns with your priorities and fits within your overall budget.

The point is that now you know, and can decide if that's how you want to allocate your resources.

Let's take a moment to address some common pitfalls, problems, issues, problems, issues in expense tracking:

1. Perfectionism: Don't let the perfect be the enemy of the good. It's okay if you miss logging an expense here and there. The goal is progress, not perfection.
2. Over-complication: While it's tempting to create dozens of specific categories, this can make the process overwhelming. Start simple and add complexity only if

needed.
3. Ignoring small expenses: That $2 vending machine snack might seem insignificant, but these small purchases can add up quickly. Log everything.
4. Failing to review and adjust: Tracking is only half the battle. Regularly review your data and use it to tell your spending decisions.
5. Forgetting about irregular expenses: Annual subscriptions, quarterly insurance payments, and other infrequent expenses can throw off your budget if you're not prepared for them. Make sure to account for these in your tracking system.

Now, let's talk tech. While the 'Receipt Revolution' method we discussed earlier is a great starting point, there's a whole world of apps and tools designed to make expense tracking easier.

Some popular options include:

- Mint: A free app that syncs with your bank accounts and automatically categorizes expenses.
- YNAB (You Need A Budget): A more hands-on approach that emphasizes planning for future expenses.
- Personal Capital: Geared towards investment tracking, and offers robust expense tracking features.
- Excel or Google Sheets: For those who prefer a DIY approach, spreadsheets offer ultimate customization.

The best tool is the one you'll actually use consistently. Try out a few and see what fits your style and needs.

Fun Fact: *The world's oldest known receipt, dating back to 2350 BC, was found in Mesopotamia and recorded the sale of clothing. Expense tracking: it's not just a modern obsession!*

It's not just about pinching pennies or impressing your accountant. It involves taking control of your financial life. It's about ensuring your money is working for you, not against you.

Every dollar you spend is a vote for the kind of life you want to live. Expense tracking simply helps you make sure those votes are going where you truly want them to.

Key Takeaways

- Consistent expense tracking is crucial for achieving financial goals
- The 'Receipt Revolution' method combines mindfulness with digital convenience
- Categorize expenses in a way that makes sense for your lifestyle
- Address cash expenses and digital subscriptions with specific strategies
- Make expense tracking a habit through gamification and accountability
- Use technology to simplify the process, but choose tools you'll actually use
- Regular review and adjustment of your tracking system is key to success
- Expense tracking is about empowerment, not restriction

CHAPTER 5: SLASHING EXPENSES WITHOUT SACRIFICING QUALITY OF LIFE

Cutting expenses is not about deprivation. It's about optimization. Every dollar you spend is a choice. It's a vote for what you value, what you prioritize, and ultimately, what kind of life you want to lead.

But here's what's interesting: most of us are terrible voters. We cast our ballots willy-nilly, swayed by flashy advertising, societal pressure, and the momentary high of retail therapy.

A life cluttered with stuff we don't need, experiences we don't truly enjoy, and a nagging feeling that our hard-earned money is slipping through our fingers like sand. It's time to become more discerning voters, to slash our expenses without feeling like we're living on bread and water.

The 'Value Optimization' approach isn't about penny-pinching until your fingers bleed. It's about ruthlessly eliminating waste while doubling down on what truly matters to you.

It's about recognizing that the latest gadget won't bring you lasting joy, but that trip to Yellowstone you've been dreaming about just might. I once thought I needed the latest smartphone to stay connected and productive. Then my trusty old flip phone died during a camping trip, and I spent a blissful week completely unplugged.

I returned home refreshed, more focused, and with a newfound skepticism about my "needs." That experience saved me thousands over the years and taught me a valuable lesson about distinguishing between wants and needs.

The beauty of this approach is it's flexibility. Your values are uniquely yours. Maybe you couldn't care less about fancy restaurants but live for live music. Perhaps you're happiest in a tiny apartment as long as it's in the heart of the city. The key is to identify what truly brings value to your life and mercilessly cut the rest.

This isn't just feel-good advice. Research backs it up. A 2019 study in the Journal of Happiness Studies found that people who focused on experiences rather than material possessions reported higher levels of life satisfaction.

Another study from the National Bureau of Economic Research revealed that households that successfully reduced expenses without feeling deprived tended to use strategic, value-based cuts rather than across-the-board slashing.

So, how do we put this into practice?

Step 1: Assess Your Current Spending

You can't improve what you don't measure. For one month, track every single penny you spend. Yes, even that $2 impulse buy at the checkout counter. Use an app, a spreadsheet, or good old-fashioned pen and paper. The method doesn't matter - the consistency does.

This exercise is often eye-opening, sometimes painfully so. You might uncover you're spending $100 a month on subscription services you barely use, or that your daily coffee habit is costing you the equivalent of a weekend getaway every few months.

Don't judge yourself during this process. The goal isn't to induce guilt but to gather data. Think of yourself as a scientist studying the fascinating spending habits of the average American consumer. It just happens that the subject is you.

Step 2: Identify Your Core Values and Priorities

Now comes the soul-searching part. What truly matters to you? What brings you joy, fulfillment, and a sense of purpose? I'm not talking about what you think should matter, but what actually does.

Maybe it's travel, education, time with family, or pursuing a creative passion. Perhaps it's building a nest egg for early retirement or having the freedom to switch careers. Whatever it is, get clear on it.

These are the areas where you'll want to allocate more resources, not less. I once worked with a client who insisted she needed to cut back on her weekly painting classes to save money. But when we dug deeper, we realized those classes were her main source of joy and stress relief.

Cutting them would have saved money at the cost of her mental health and overall life satisfaction. Instead, we found other areas to trim that had less impact on her well-being.

Step 3: Categorize Your Expenses

Armed with your spending data and a clear understanding of your values, it's time to sort your expenses into three categories:

1. Essential: These are the non-negotiables. Housing, food, utilities, healthcare, and any debt payments fall here.
2. Important: These align with your core values and priorities but aren't absolute necessities. This might include your gym membership if health is a top priority, or your Netflix

subscription if unwinding with a good show is crucial to your mental health.
3. Optional: Everything else. Be ruthless here. Just because something has always been part of your budget doesn't mean it deserves to stay.

Step 4: The Great Expense Purge

Now comes the fun part (yes, I said fun – embrace your inner financial nerd). Start with the "Optional" category and ask yourself these questions for each expense:

- Does this align with my core values and priorities?
- Does the joy or utility I get from this justify the cost?
- Is there a less expensive way to get the same benefit?

Be prepared for some tough decisions. That fancy gym membership might need to go in favor of home workouts and runs in the park. The daily latte might become a once-a-week treat. Your cable package might get downgraded or cut entirely in favor of a single streaming service.

This isn't about depriving yourself. It's about reallocating resources to what truly matters. Every dollar you save on things you don't really care about is a dollar you can put toward what you do care about.

Step 5: Optimize the Essentials

Just because something is essential doesn't mean there isn't room for optimization. Let's break down some major categories:

Housing: This is often the biggest expense in most budgets. Could you downsize? Get a roommate? Negotiate your rent? If you own, could you refinance for a better rate? A smaller space often means lower utility bills and less money spent on furnishings and maintenance.

Food: Meal planning, buying in bulk, and cooking at home can dramatically cut food costs without sacrificing nutrition or taste. Learn to cook a few signature dishes that are both delicious and budget-friendly. Your wallet and your waistline will thank you.

Transportation: Could you carpool, use public transit, or bike more often? If you have two cars, could you downsize to one? If you're in the market for a new vehicle, consider the total cost of ownership, not just the sticker price.

Utilities: Simple changes like using LED bulbs, adjusting your thermostat, and fixing leaky faucets can add up to significant savings over time.

Step 6: The Art of Negotiation

Many people don't realize how many of their regular bills are negotiable. Cable, internet, cell phone plans, insurance premiums – all of these can often be reduced with a simple phone call. The key is to do your homework. Research competitor rates and be prepared to switch if necessary.

Be polite but firm. These companies want to keep your business. I once saved $600 a year on my internet bill with a 15-minute phone call. The secret? I had researched a competitor's offer and was prepared to switch. Suddenly, my "locked-in" rate became very flexible.

Step 7: Embrace the Sharing Economy

We live in an age of unprecedented access to goods and services without the need for ownership. Need a power tool for a one-time project? Rent it or borrow it from a neighbor. Want to read more but don't want to buy books? Your local library is free knowledge and entertainment.

Platforms like Airbnb, Turo, and TaskRabbit have made it easier than ever to monetize your assets and skills. Could you rent out a spare room occasionally? Use your car for ridesharing on weekends? These "side hustles" can help offset your expenses without requiring a huge time commitment.

Step 8: Find Free or Low-Cost Alternatives

Entertainment and self-care are crucial for a good quality of life, but they don't have to break the bank. Museums often have free days. Parks and nature trails offer free recreation. YouTube is a goldmine of free workouts, meditation guides, and educational content.

For social activities, consider hosting potluck dinners instead of eating out. Organize a clothing swap with friends instead of a shopping spree. Get creative – often, the most memorable experiences are the ones that cost the least.

Key Insight: *The 'latte factor,' coined by financial author David Bach, suggests that small daily expenses can significantly impact long-term savings. That $4 daily coffee habit adds up to over $1,400 a year – enough for a nice vacation or a substantial contribution to your retirement fund.*

Step 9: Adopt Minimalist Principles

Minimalism isn't about living in a bare white room with a single chair. It's about being intentional with your possessions and your spending. It's about recognizing that more stuff doesn't equal more happiness.

Start by decluttering. Sell or donate items you no longer use or love. Not only will this potentially bring in some extra cash, but it will also make you more mindful of future purchases. Before buying something new, ask yourself: "Do I really need this? Will it truly add value to my life?"

This mindset shift can be profound. You'll likely find yourself spending less not because you're depriving yourself, but because you're more selective about what you allow into your life.

Step 10: Track, Adjust, and Celebrate

Implementing these changes is just the beginning. The key to long-term success is to track your progress, adjust as needed, and celebrate your wins.
Set up a system to watch your spending regularly. This could be as simple as a monthly review of your bank statements or as detailed as maintaining a daily spending log. The important thing is to stay aware of where your money is going.

Be prepared to make adjustments. Maybe you cut too deep in one area and need to allocate a bit more. Or perhaps you uncover new areas where you can optimize. This is a process, not a one-time event. Most importantly, celebrate your progress. Did you hit your savings goal for the month? Treat yourself to something you enjoy (within reason, of course).

Did you successfully negotiate a bill? Do a victory dance in your living room. Positive reinforcement will help make these new habits stick.

The goal of all this isn't to have the lowest possible expenses. It's to create a life that aligns with your values and brings you joy and fulfillment. If you're spending less overall but feeling more satisfied with your life, you're doing it right.

Interesting Fact: The concept of 'voluntary simplicity' dates back to ancient Greek and Roman philosophers who advocated for living with less to achieve greater happiness. In our modern consumer-driven society, this ancient wisdom is more relevant than ever.

Key Takeaways

- Cutting expenses is about optimizing your spending, not depriving yourself.
- Identify your core values and priorities to guide your spending decisions.
- Track all expenses and categorize them as essential, important, or optional.
- Be ruthless in cutting optional expenses that don't align with your values.
- Optimize essential expenses through research and negotiation.
- Embrace the sharing economy and free or low-cost alternatives for entertainment and self-care.
- Adopt minimalist principles to reduce clutter and mindless spending.
- Regularly track your progress, adjust as needed, and celebrate your wins.
- the goal is to create a life that brings you joy and fulfillment, not just to spend as little as possible.

CHAPTER 6: BOOSTING YOUR INCOME - BECAUSE EARNING MORE MATTERS TOO

Money, as they say, doesn't grow on trees. But wouldn't it be nice if it did? Imagine strolling through your backyard, plucking crisp $100 bills from the branches of a money tree. Alas, the reality is far less arboreal and far more arduous. Yet, while we can't cultivate currency in our gardens, we can certainly cultivate our earning potential.

In our quest for financial stability and growth, we often focus on trimming expenses, pinching pennies, and squeezing every last drop of value from our hard-earned cash. But there's another side to this fiscal coin – boosting our income. It's like trying to fill a bathtub - sure, you can plug the drain to stop the water from escaping, but at some point, you've got to turn on the faucet if you want to take a proper bath.

Increasing your income isn't about having more money to splurge on fancy dinners or the latest gadgets (though that's certainly a perk). It involves creating financial security, building a safety net, and opening doors to opportunities that might otherwise stay firmly shut.

It's about giving yourself the freedom to make choices based on what you want, rather than what you can afford. But here's what's interesting – boosting your income doesn't necessarily mean working yourself to the bone or selling your soul to the corporate devil. In fact, some of the most effective ways to increase your earnings can be downright enjoyable.

The landscape of earning has changed dramatically over the

past few decades. Gone are the days when a single income stream was enough to support a comfortable lifestyle. Today, the average millionaire has seven streams of income.

Seven! That's not just a stream - it's a whole darn river delta of cash flow. This shift towards multiple income streams isn't just for the wealthy elite. A 2019 Bankrate survey revealed that 45% of Americans have a side hustle. That's nearly half the country moonlighting as Uber drivers, freelance writers, dog walkers, or any number of other income-generating activities.

And there's more to it than just making ends meet – many people are using these extra income streams to fund their dreams, pay off debt faster, or simply enjoy a little more financial breathing room. But before you start panicking about how you're going to juggle seven different jobs, take a deep breath. We're not talking about working 24/7 or turning into some sort of income-generating robot.

Instead, we're going to explore smart, strategic ways to boost your earnings without losing your sanity in the process.

Let's start with your primary income source – your job. Many people make the mistake of thinking their salary is set in stone, as immovable as a stubborn mule. But that's simply not true. Your earning potential at your current job is often far more flexible than you might think.

First things first – when was the last time you asked for a raise? If you're like most people, the answer is probably "not recently enough." Many of us shy away from these conversations, fearing rejection or awkwardness.

But here's a little secret: your boss isn't a mind reader. If you don't ask for a raise, you're far less likely to get one. Before you march into your boss's office demanding more money, though, do your homework. Research the average salary for your position in your area. Sites like Glassdoor, Payscale, and Salary.com can be invaluable resources for this.

Then, make a list of your accomplishments over the past year. Have you taken on extra responsibilities? Brought in new clients? Streamlined a process that saved the company money? These are all excellent bargaining chips. When you do have the conversation, frame it in terms of value. Don't focus on why you need more money (your boss doesn't care that your cat needs expensive dental surgery).

Instead, emphasize the value you bring to the company and how your contributions justify a higher salary. But what if you've maxed out your earning potential at your current job? It might be time to look for greener pastures. Job-hopping, once seen as a career faux pas, is now recognized as one of the most effective ways to increase your earnings.

A Forbes study found that employees who stay at a company for more than two years earn 50% less over their lifetime compared to those who change jobs more often. Of course, changing jobs isn't always feasible or desirable. That's where the concept of the 'side hustle' comes in.

The term 'side hustle' gained popularity in the 1950s among African American communities as a way to describe extra work to supplement income. Today, it's become a cultural phenomenon, with people of all backgrounds embracing the idea of multiple income streams.

Key Idea: The 'Skill Stack' Method
Instead of becoming an expert in one narrow field, develop a unique combination of complementary skills. This 'skill stack' can make you more valuable in your current job and open up new income opportunities.

For example, a graphic designer who also understands marketing and basic coding can offer more comprehensive services to clients.

But where do you start? The key is to leverage your existing skills and interests. Are you a whiz with words? Consider freelance writing or editing. Have a knack for numbers? Bookkeeping or tax preparation services could be your ticket. Love animals? Dog walking or pet sitting might be right up your alley.

One of the beauties of the modern age is the plethora of platforms available to connect you with potential clients. Sites like Upwork, Fiverr, and Freelancer.com allow you to offer your services to a global market.

If you're more product-oriented, platforms like Etsy or Shopify can help you set up an online store with minimal fuss. Speaking of products, let's talk about turning hobbies into cold, hard cash. We've all heard the advice "do what you love and you'll never work a day in your life." While that might be a bit of an exaggeration (even dream jobs have their tedious moments), there's certainly something to be said for monetizing your passions.

Take knitting, for example. You might think it's just a way to keep your hands busy while binging Netflix, but the handmade market is booming. Etsy, the go-to platform for handmade goods, reported $3.93 billion in gross merchandise sales in 2018. That's a lot of hand-knitted scarves and artisanal soap.

But maybe crafts aren't your thing. Perhaps you're more of a tech enthusiast. Did you know that you can make money testing websites and apps? Companies are always looking for fresh eyes to spot usability issues, and they're willing to pay for it. Sites like UserTesting and TestingTime connect companies with testers, and you can earn anywhere from $10 to $60 per test.

Or maybe you're sitting on a goldmine of knowledge without even realizing it. Are you fluent in a second language? Sites like VIPKid and italki allow you to teach language lessons online. Have expertise in a particular subject? Create an online course on platforms like Udemy or Teachable. The e-learning market is projected to reach $325 billion by 2025, so there's plenty of pie to go around.

Now, I know what you're thinking. "This all sounds great, but I barely have time to do my laundry, let alone start a side business." Time management is indeed one of the biggest challenges when it comes to increasing your income. But here's where we need to shift our perspective a bit.

Think of your time like your money – it's a resource to be invested wisely. Just as you might cut back on unnecessary expenses to save money, you might need to cut back on time-wasters to free up hours for income-generating activities. This might mean saying no to that Netflix binge session, or waking up an hour earlier each day. It might mean outsourcing some tasks to free up your time for higher-value activities.

Yes, paying someone to mow your lawn or clean your house might seem counterintuitive when you're trying to make more money, but if it frees you up to earn significantly more through your side hustle, it's a smart investment.

One strategy that can be particularly effective is the 'time blocking' method. Instead of trying to multitask (which, studies show, actually decreases productivity), dedicate specific blocks of time to specific tasks. Maybe Tuesday and Thursday evenings are for your freelance work, while Saturday mornings are for developing your online course.

But what about the financial side of managing multiple income streams? This is where things can get a bit tricky, especially when it comes to taxes. When you're earning income from multiple sources, particularly if you're doing freelance or contract work, you're responsible for setting aside money for taxes. A good rule of thumb is to save about 30% of your extra income for taxes.

It's also crucial to keep meticulous records of your income and expenses related to your side hustles. Not only will this make tax time less of a headache, but it will also help you see which of your income-generating activities are truly worth your time and effort.

Interesting Fact *The concept of multiple income streams dates back to ancient civilizations. Farmers would often engage in crafts during off-seasons to supplement their income. The more things change, the more they stay the same!*

Now, let's talk about scaling. Once you've got your side hustle up and running, how do you take it to the next level? This is where the 'Micro-Entrepreneurship' approach comes in handy. Instead of trying to build a massive business overnight, focus on small, manageable growth.

For instance, if you're doing freelance graphic design, you might start by taking on one or two clients. As you build your portfolio and reputation, you can gradually increase your rates and take on more work. Eventually, you might even be able to outsource some of the work, turning your side hustle into a small business.

But scaling isn't about doing more of the same. It's also about finding ways to leverage your efforts for greater returns. This is where passive income streams come into play. Passive income is money earned with minimal ongoing effort. It's the holy grail of income boosting – making money while you sleep.

Creating truly passive income often needs significant upfront effort, but the long-term payoff can be substantial. Writing and self-publishing an e-book, creating a popular YouTube channel, or developing a mobile app are all examples of potentially passive income streams.

One particularly interesting approach is the concept of 'digital real estate.' This involves creating valuable online assets that generate ongoing income. For example, you might create a niche website that earns money through advertising or affiliate marketing.

Once the site is established and ranking well in search engines, it can continue to generate income with minimal ongoing work. Of course, no discussion of income boosting would be finish without addressing the elephant in the room – the gig economy. Companies like Uber, Lyft, DoorDash, and Instacart have created unprecedented opportunities for flexible, on-demand work.

While these gigs might not make you rich, they can be an excellent way to supplement your income on your own schedule. But here's a word of caution – the gig economy isn't all sunshine and rainbows. These jobs often come with hidden costs (wear and tear on your car, for instance) and lack the benefits and stability of traditional employment. They can be a great stopgap or supplementary income source, but be wary of relying on them too heavily.

As we wrap up this whirlwind tour of income boosting strategies, let's take a moment to address some common pitfalls, problems, issues. First and foremost, beware of get-rich-quick schemes. If something sounds too good to be true, it probably is.

Building extra income streams takes time and effort – anyone promising overnight riches is likely trying to separate you from your money, not help you make more.

Another common mistake is neglecting self-care if you're targeting more income. Yes, hustling is important, but burning yourself out won't do you any favors in the long run. Make sure to build in time for rest, relaxation, and activities that recharge your batteries.

Finally, don't forget about the importance of continuous learning. The job market and the economy are constantly evolving, and staying relevant means constantly updating your skills. Invest in yourself through courses, workshops, or even just reading widely in your field. You are your own most valuable asset.

Boosting your income isn't about making more money – this involves creating more opportunities, more security, and more freedom in your life. Whether you're negotiating a raise, starting a side hustle, or building passive income streams, every step you take towards increasing your earnings is a step towards a more financially stable future.

Money might not grow on trees, but with the right strategies and a bit of hustle, you can certainly make it bloom.

Key Takeaways:

- Your salary isn't set in stone – don't be afraid to negotiate for what you're worth
- Multiple income streams provide financial stability and opportunities
- Side hustles can be both profitable and enjoyable when aligned with your skills and interests

- Time management is crucial – invest your time wisely
- Passive income streams can provide long-term financial benefits
- Continuous learning and skill development are key to increasing your earning potential
- Beware of get-rich-quick schemes and burnout
- Increasing your income is about creating more opportunities and financial freedom

CHAPTER 7: DEBT DEMOLITION - STRATEGIES FOR BECOMING DEBT-FREE

I know that it can often seem like debt is an inescapable part of modern life. But the hard fact is that the only way you can truly achieve financial freedom is by tackling your debts head-on and developing a solid strategy to become debt-free.

Some people can manage their debts without too much stress, and if you think that's your situation, then you might be tempted to let things ride. But most people find that debt becomes an ever-increasing burden, weighing them down financially and emotionally.

If you're feeling overwhelmed by debt, then you're spending more money on interest and repayments than you can comfortably afford. We accumulate debt from various sources - credit cards, personal loans, mortgages, and even those insidious "buy now, pay later" schemes that seem to pop up everywhere these days.

Debt, much like a clingy ex-partner, has a nasty habit of sticking around long after it's welcome has worn out. It's the uninvited guest at your financial dinner party, always asking for seconds and never offering to do the dishes. But don't worry, dear reader, for we're about to set off on a journey to kick debt to the curb and reclaim your financial freedom.

Now, before we dive into the nitty-gritty of debt demolition, let's take a moment to appreciate the sheer absurdity of our modern relationship with debt. We live in what happens when it's perfectly normal to spend money we don't have on things we don't need, to impress people we don't even like.

It's as if we've collectively decided that future-us will be so much richer and more responsible that they'll happily clean up our financial messes. Spoiler alert: future-you is just as broke and irresponsible as present-you, only with more wrinkles and a growing resentment towards past-you.

But I digress. The point is, debt has become so normalized that we often fail to recognize it's true cost on our financial health. It's like that slow-growing mold in the corner of your bathroom - you might not notice it day-to-day, but before you know it, it's taken over and you're wondering why everything smells funky.

The true cost of debt goes far beyond the numbers on your credit card statement. It's the stress that keeps you up at night, the opportunities you have to pass up because you're too busy paying off past purchases, and the constant feeling that you're running on a financial treadmill, exhausted but getting nowhere.

Debt affects your credit score, which in turn impacts your ability to secure loans, rent apartments, and sometimes even land jobs. It's the gift that keeps on taking, long after you've forgotten what you spent the money on in the first place. Remember that overpriced avocado toast you bought three years ago?

Well, if you put it on a credit card and haven't paid it off, you're still paying for it. And let me tell you, no avocado toast is worth three years of compound interest. But enough doom and gloom. The good news is that becoming debt-free is possible, it's also incredibly rewarding.

Here's a life where your paycheck is actually yours to keep, where you can save for the future instead of paying for the past, and where the only thing keeping you up at night is your neighbor's questionable taste in late-night karaoke songs.

Now, let's talk strategy. When it comes to paying off debt, there are two main schools of thought: the Debt Snowball method and the Debt Avalanche method. These aren't cute names for winter sports, but rather different approaches to tackling your debt.

The Debt Snowball method, popularized by financial guru Dave Ramsey, is all about the psychological win. You start by paying off your smallest debt first, regardless of interest rate. The idea is that by quickly eliminating a debt entirely, you'll get a boost of motivation that will help you tackle the bigger debts. It's like starting your diet by giving up celery - sure, it's not making a huge difference, but boy does it feel good to check something off the list.

On the other hand, the Debt Avalanche method is for those of you who prefer cold, hard math to warm, fuzzy feelings. With this approach, you focus on paying off the debt with the highest interest rate first, regardless of the balance. This method will save you more money in the long run, as you're tackling the most expensive debt first. It's the financial equivalent of eating your vegetables before dessert - not as immediately satisfying, but better for you in the long run.

So which method should you choose? Well, that depends on whether you're more motivated by quick wins or long-term savings. If you're the type of person who needs regular pats on the back to stay motivated, the Snowball method might be for you. If you're more of a numbers person who gets a thrill from minimizing interest payments, then the Avalanche method is your jam.

Personally, I'm a fan of the hybrid approach. Start with the Snowball method to build momentum, then switch to the

Avalanche once you've got a few wins under your belt. It's like starting your workout with a brisk walk before breaking into a full sprint - you warm up your motivation muscles before tackling the tough stuff.

Now, whichever method you choose, the key is to create a debt repayment plan that fits your budget. And speaking of budgets, if you don't have one yet, it's time to make one. I know, I know, budgeting is about as exciting as watching paint dry. But trust me, it's a lot more fun than drowning in debt.

Start by listing all your debts, including the balance, interest rate, and least payment for each. Then, look at your income and expenses. Be honest with yourself here - that daily latte habit isn't fooling anyone. Once you've got a clear picture of your financial situation, it's time to get creative about freeing up extra cash to throw at your debt.

This might mean cutting back on non-essential expenses (goodbye, subscription to the Cheese of the Month Club), finding ways to increase your income (hello, side hustle), or both. Every extra dollar you can put towards your debt is a dollar that won't be charging you interest in the future.

One common mistake people make when trying to become debt-free is not accounting for unexpected expenses. Life has a funny way of throwing financial curveballs when you least expect them. Your car breaks down, your pet needs emergency surgery, or you suddenly realize you can't go another day without replacing your lumpy mattress.

If you don't have an emergency fund, these unexpected costs can derail your debt repayment plan faster than you can say "credit card debt." To avoid this, try to build a small emergency fund even as you're paying off debt. Aim for at least $1,000 to start - enough to cover most minor emergencies without having to rely on credit. Once you've got that safety net in place, you can focus on demolishing your debt without constantly looking over your shoulder for the next financial disaster.

Another pitfall, problem, issue, problem, issue to watch out for is the temptation to use debt consolidation as a quick fix. While consolidating your debts into a single, lower-interest loan can be a smart move in some cases, it's not a magic solution. If you don't address the underlying habits that got you into debt in the first place, you'll likely find yourself right back where you started, only with a shiny new consolidation loan on top of your old debts.

Key Insight: *Debt consolidation can be a useful tool, but it's not a substitute for changing your financial habits. It's like putting a Band-Aid on a broken leg - it might look better, but it doesn't solve the underlying problem.*

Now, let's talk about staying motivated on your debt-free journey. Paying off debt can feel like a long, uphill battle, especially if you've got a significant amount to tackle. It's easy to get discouraged when it seems like you're not making progress, or when you see your friends living it up while you're eating ramen for the third night in a row.

One way to stay motivated is to celebrate your wins, no matter how small. Paid off a credit card? Do a happy dance in your living room. Reached 25% of your debt-free goal? Treat yourself to a movie night (at home, with microwave popcorn, because we're being financially responsible here). The point is to acknowledge your progress and remind yourself why you're doing this in the first place.

Another motivational trick is to visualize your debt-free future. What will you do with all that extra money once you're not sending it to creditors every month? Maybe you'll finally take that dream vacation, start saving for a house, or just enjoy the peace of mind that comes with financial freedom.

Whatever your goal, keep it front and center. Some people even create vision boards or set a picture of their dream destination as their phone background. Just make sure it's not a picture of something you'll be tempted to buy on credit.

Becoming debt-free is a marathon, not a sprint. There will be times when you feel like you're making great progress, and times when it feels like you're running in place. The key is to keep moving forward, even if it's just baby steps.

Arguably the most potent resource in your debt-demolition arsenal is the art of negotiation. Many people don't realize that credit card interest rates and even some loan terms are negotiable. It never hurts to call your creditors and ask for a lower interest rate, especially if you've been making your payments on time. The worst they can say is no, and the best case scenario could save you hundreds or even thousands in interest.

When you make these calls, be polite but firm. Explain that you're committed to paying off your debt and that you've been offered lower rates by other creditors (even if you haven't - a little white lie in the service of financial freedom never hurt anyone). You might be surprised at how often they're willing to work with you, especially if the alternative is you transferring your balance to another card.

Speaking of balance transfers, these can be a useful tool in your debt repayment strategy, but they come with their own set of pitfalls, problems, issues. Many cards offer promotional 0% interest rates on balance transfers, which can save you a bundle in interest if you're able to pay off the balance before the promotional period ends. However, be sure to read the fine print

- there's often a balance transfer fee, and if you don't pay off the balance in time, you could be hit with retroactive interest.

As you're working on becoming debt-free, it's crucial to avoid taking on new debt. This might seem obvious, but it's easier said than done, especially if you're used to relying on credit cards for everyday expenses or emergencies.

One strategy is to literally freeze your credit cards - put them in a container of water and stick them in the freezer. This creates a literal and figurative barrier between you and impulse purchases. By the time the ice thaws, you'll have had plenty of time to reconsider whether you really need that new gadget or designer handbag.

Fun Fact: The average American household carries $6,270 in credit card debt. If that doesn't motivate you to pay off your debts, consider this: if you only made the least payment on that balance, it would take you over 17 years to pay it off, and you'd end up paying more in interest than the original balance. That's like buying everything twice!

Now, let's talk about the elephant in the room - or should I say, the debt-shaped monster under the bed. Many people avoid dealing with their debt because they're afraid to face the full extent of what they owe.

It's like that pile of laundry in the corner of your bedroom that you keep adding to, hoping that if you ignore it long enough, it'll magically clean itself. Spoiler alert: it won't, and neither will your debt.

The first step in conquering your debt is to face it head-on. Gather all your statements, log into all your accounts, and write down every single debt you have, no matter how small or embarrassing. Yes, even that $50 you still owe your brother-in-law from that ill-advised poker night three Christmases ago.

Getting a clear picture of your total debt can be scary, but it's also empowering. You can't fight an enemy you can't see, and you can't conquer a debt you're pretending doesn't exist. Once you've got your debt laid out in front of you, it's time to prioritize. This is where the Snowball vs. Avalanche debate comes into play again.

There's no one-size-fits-all approach here. The best method is the one you'll actually stick to. If you need those quick wins to stay motivated, start with your smallest debt. If you're all about efficiency and minimizing interest, tackle the highest interest rate first.

As you're working on paying off your debt, it's important to keep an eye on your credit score. Your credit score is like your financial report card, and unfortunately, it doesn't go away after you graduate. Lenders, landlords, and even some employers use it to gauge your financial responsibility. The good news is that as you pay down your debt, your credit score is likely to improve.

However, be aware that closing credit card accounts after you've paid them off can actually hurt your credit score in the short term. This is because it reduces your available credit, which can increase your credit utilization ratio (the amount of credit you're using compared to your total available credit). If possible, keep your old accounts open, but resist the temptation to use them.

Think of them like that treadmill you bought with the best intentions - it's better to have it and not use it than to get rid of it and regret it later. Now, let's address one of the biggest obstacles to becoming debt-free: lifestyle inflation. This is the tendency to increase your spending as your income increases.

Got a raise? Time for a new car! Bonus at work? Let's upgrade to the latest smartphone!

This kind of thinking is what keeps many people trapped in the cycle of debt. Instead of automatically increasing your spending when your income goes up, challenge yourself to maintain your current lifestyle and put the extra money towards your debt. It's like finding money in your coat pocket, except instead of treating yourself to lunch, you're treating yourself to financial freedom. Trust me, future-you will be much more grateful for a debt-free life than for that fancy lunch you've already forgotten about.

As you're working on becoming debt-free, it's important to surround yourself with supportive people. This might mean finding a debt-free community online, or simply being open with your friends and family about your financial goals. You don't have to broadcast your debt to the world, but having a support system can make a big difference when you're feeling tempted to splurge or discouraged by slow progress.

Becoming debt-free is about a lot more than just the numbers - this involves changing your relationship with money. It involves learning to live within your means, to distinguish between wants and needs, and to find satisfaction in financial security as opposed to material possessions. It's a blueprint that leads towards self-discovery as much as it is a blueprint that leads towards financial improvement.

And speaking of journeys, let's talk about the light at the end of the tunnel. Becoming debt-free is not about getting rid of a financial burden - this involves opening up a world of possibilities. When you're not sending a chunk of your paycheck to creditors every month, you have the freedom to save for the future, invest in yourself, or pursue passions that you've been putting off.

Imagine being able to take that dream vacation without worrying about how you'll pay for it when you get back. Visualize yourself starting a business, going back to school, or retiring early - all because you're not weighed down by debt. That's the kind of freedom that makes all the budgeting, sacrificing, and hard work worth it.

So, as you set off on your debt-free journey, remember: every payment you make is a step towards freedom. Every impulse purchase you resist is a victory. And every dollar of debt you pay off is a dollar that's working for you, not against you.

Here's a summary of key takeaways to keep in mind as you work towards becoming debt-free:

- Understand the true cost of your debt - it's more than just the balance on your statement
- Choose a debt repayment strategy that works for you, whether it's the Snowball method, Avalanche method, or a hybrid approach
- Create a realistic budget and look for ways to free up extra cash for debt repayment
- Build a small emergency fund to avoid relying on credit for unexpected expenses
- Be cautious with debt consolidation - it's a tool, not a solution
- Celebrate your wins, no matter how small, to stay motivated
- Visualize your debt-free future to keep your eyes on the prize
- Don't be afraid to negotiate with creditors for better terms
- Avoid taking on new debt while you're paying off existing debt

- Face your total debt head-on - you can't conquer what you can't see
- Be mindful of lifestyle inflation and resist the urge to increase spending as your income grows
- Surround yourself with supportive people who understand your financial goals
- Remember that becoming debt-free is about changing your relationship with money, not just about the numbers
- Keep your eye on the freedom and possibilities that await you in a debt-free life

CHAPTER 8: BUILDING YOUR FINANCIAL FORTRESS - SAVING AND INVESTING

Before we can teach you how to build a financial fortress that will withstand the storms of life, we need to settle the question of what truly constitutes financial security. The obvious answer is that financial security means having enough money to cover your needs and wants without constant worry. But what does that look like in practice?

Surprisingly, there's very little consensus on what constitutes true financial security. Almost all the financial advice you see reported in the media is about the benefits of this or that new investment strategy or get-rich-quick scheme. Since none of these strategies or schemes actually lead to long-term wealth for most people, they're careful to avoid connecting their methods with real, sustainable financial security.

The studies that do connect saving and investing habits to long-term financial well-being rarely make their way into the popular press. To find them, you must comb through obscure academic journals or explore the annals of economic research.

But don't worry, intrepid reader! I've done the hard work for you, sifting through mountains of financial gobbledygook to bring you the essence of what it truly means to build a financial fortress. And let me tell you, it's not about finding the next hot stock or cryptocurrency.

It's about laying a solid foundation, brick by brick, until you've created a structure so sturdy that even the big bad wolf of economic downturns can't blow it down. Now, I know what you're thinking. "Great, another lecture about pinching pennies and giving up my daily latte." But hold onto your overpriced coffee cups, because that's not what we're here for. Building a financial fortress isn't about deprivation – this involves smart allocation of resources and making your money work as hard as you do.

Let's start with the cornerstone of any solid financial structure: the emergency fund. If you don't have one, you're essentially living in a financial house of cards, just waiting for a strong gust of wind (or an unexpected car repair) to bring it all tumbling down. An emergency fund is your financial shock absorber. It's what stands between you and the dreaded high-interest credit card debt when life throws you a curveball. And let's face it, life is basically a professional baseball pitcher when it comes to curveballs.

So, how much should you squirrel away in this magical money cushion? The general rule of thumb is three to six months of living expenses. But like all rules of thumb, this one assumes you have an average number of thumbs. Your personal situation might call for more or less.

If you're a freelancer with an irregular income, for instance, you might want to aim for the higher end of that range, or even beyond. On the other hand, if you have a stable job in a recession-proof industry (do those even exist anymore?), you might be comfortable with a smaller buffer.

The key is to start somewhere. Even $500 set aside can be the difference between a minor inconvenience and a financial catastrophe. So, start small if you must, but start.

Now, let's talk about the magic of automation. If you're relying on willpower alone to save money, you're fighting an uphill battle. Willpower is like a muscle – it gets fatigued with overuse. That's why you're more likely to blow your diet at the end of a long, stressful day. The solution? Make saving as automatic as possible. Set up direct deposits from your paycheck into your savings account. Treat it like a bill that must be paid. Because in a way, it is – you're paying your future self.

This strategy takes advantage of a psychological quirk known as "out of sight, out of mind." If the money never hits your checking account, you're less likely to miss it. It's like financial sleight of hand, only you're the magician and the audience. But saving is only half the battle. To truly build wealth, you need to make your money work for you. That's where investing comes in.

Now, I know the word "investing" might conjure images of Wall Street bros in pinstripe suits, yelling "Buy! Sell!" into multiple phones at once. But in reality, smart investing for the average person is much less dramatic and much more boring. The key to successful long-term investing is diversification and patience. It's not about trying to time the market or pick the next Amazon.

It's about consistently putting money into a mix of low-cost index funds that track the overall market. Why index funds? Because they offer broad exposure to the market at a low cost. And here's a dirty little secret of the financial world: most actively managed funds (the ones where highly paid managers try to beat the market) actually underperform simple index funds over the long term.

Key Idea: *The power of compound interest is often called the eighth wonder of the world. Albert Einstein supposedly said, "He who understands it, earns it - he who doesn't, pays it." Whether Einstein actually said this is debatable, but the principle holds true. Start investing early, and let time do the heavy lifting for you.*

Now, I can almost hear some of you protesting. "But what

about crypto? What about that hot new tech stock my cousin's roommate's dog walker told me about?" To which I say: by all means, if you want to gamble with a small portion of your portfolio, go ahead. But treat it like you would a trip to Vegas – only play with money you can afford to lose.

The bulk of your investments should be boring. Boringly effective. Like a dependable old station wagon that always starts on the first try, not a flashy sports car that spends half it's time in the shop.

But what about balancing saving for the future with enjoying life now? This is where the concept of the "Opportunity Fund" comes in. This is separate from your emergency fund and your retirement savings. It's money you set aside for big goals or experiences – maybe a dream vacation, a down payment on a house, or starting your own business.

The Opportunity Fund is your "yes" fund. It allows you to say yes to life's big opportunities without derailing your long-term financial plans or going into debt. It's the financial equivalent of having your cake and eating it too. To build your Opportunity Fund, start by identifying your big goals. Then, just like with your emergency fund and retirement savings, automate contributions to this fund. Even small, regular contributions can add up over time.

The goal isn't to live like a miser now so you can be rich later. It's about finding a balance that allows you to enjoy life now while also building for the future. Now, let's talk about one of the biggest financial challenges many people face: balancing saving for retirement with current expenses. It's easy to put off saving for retirement when it feels so far away and you have bills staring you in the face right now.

But, thanks to the magic of compound interest, every year you delay saving for retirement costs you dearly in the long run. A dollar saved in your 20s can be worth ten times as much as a dollar saved in your 50s by the time you retire. So how do you balance these competing priorities? The key is to start small and increase your savings rate over time.

Many financial experts recommend the "50/30/20" rule as a starting point. This means allocating 50% of your income to needs, 30% to wants, and 20% to savings and debt repayment. If 20% feels impossible right now, start with whatever you can – even if it's just 1% of your income. Then, commit to increasing your savings rate by 1% every few months. You'll barely notice the difference in your paycheck, but over time, it can make a huge difference in your savings.

Another strategy is to "pay yourself first." This means treating your savings like a non-negotiable expense, just like your rent or utilities. Set up automatic transfers to your savings and investment accounts as soon as your paycheck hits your account. Then, learn to live on what's left. This might sound daunting, but remember: you're not depriving yourself. You're paying your future self. And your future self will thank you profusely.

Now, let's address a common concern: "Is it too late to start saving for retirement if I'm in my 40s or 50s?" The short answer is no. The best time to start saving was 20 years ago. The second-best time is now. If you're getting a late start, you might need to save more aggressively. You might also need to rethink your retirement plans.

Maybe you'll work a few years longer, or maybe you'll downsize your lifestyle in retirement. But the key is to start now and save as much as you can. It's not all or nothing. Every dollar you save now is a dollar (plus interest) you'll have in retirement. And that's better than nothing.

Let's talk about a concept that's crucial for long-term financial success: the difference between saving and investing. While these terms are often used interchangeably, they represent two distinct strategies for managing your money. Saving typically refers to setting aside money in a safe, easily accessible account – like a savings account at your bank. This money is for short-term goals or emergencies. It's not meant to grow significantly - it's primary purpose is to be there when you need it.

Investing, on the other hand, is about putting your money to work with the goal of growing it over time. This usually involves buying assets like stocks, bonds, or real estate that have the potential to increase in value. Investing comes with more risk than saving, and the potential for higher returns. Think of it this way: saving is like putting your money in a safe. It's secure, but it's not doing much while it's in there. Investing is like planting seeds. There's a risk that some won't grow, but those that do can multiply your initial investment many times over.

Both saving and investing are crucial parts of a solid financial plan. Your emergency fund and short-term savings should be in easily accessible, low-risk accounts. But for long-term goals like retirement, you'll likely need the growth potential that comes with investing.

Now, I know what some of you are thinking: "Investing sounds great, but I barely have two nickels to rub together. How am I supposed to start investing?" Good news: you don't need a fortune to start investing. Many mutual funds and exchange-traded funds (ETFs) allow you to start with as little as $50 or $100. Some newer investing apps even let you invest spare change from your everyday purchases.

The key is to start small and be consistent. Even $25 a

week invested regularly can grow to a substantial sum over time, thanks to the magic of compound returns. Speaking of compound returns, let's take a moment to appreciate just how powerful this concept is. Compound returns occur when you earn returns not just on your initial investment, and on the returns from previous years.

To illustrate this, let's consider two hypothetical investors: Early Bird Emily and Latecomer Larry. Emily starts investing $200 a month at age 25. Larry waits until he's 35 to start, but invests $400 a month to make up for lost time. Both invest until they're 65.

Assuming an average annual return of 7% (which is in line with historical stock market returns), Emily would end up with about $525,000, while Larry would have about $465,000. Even though Larry invested more in total ($144,000 vs Emily's $96,000), he ended up with less because he missed out on those crucial early years of compound growth.

This isn't to discourage those getting a late start – remember, the best time to start is now, regardless of your age. But it does illustrate the immense power of starting early and letting compound returns work their magic.

Key Insight: *The Rule of 72 is a quick way to estimate how long it will take for an investment to double. Simply divide 72 by the annual rate of return.*
For example, at a 7% return, an investment will double in about 10 years (72 ÷ 7 = 10.3). This rule can help you quickly gauge the potential growth of your investments.

Now, let's address one of the most common dilemmas people face when trying to improve their financial situation: should you pay off debt or start investing? The answer, as with many things in personal finance, is: it depends. If you have high-interest debt (like credit card debt), it usually makes sense to focus on paying that off first. The interest you're paying on that debt is likely higher than any returns you could reliably earn from investing.

However, if you have low-interest debt (like a mortgage), it might make sense to start investing while you're paying off the debt. This is especially true if you have access to a 401(k) with employer matching. That match is essentially free money – an instant 100% return on your investment. It's hard to beat that.

The ideal scenario, of course, is to do both: pay down debt and invest. But if you're just starting out and resources are tight, focus on building an emergency fund first, then tackle high-interest debt, and then start investing.

Personal finance is personal. What works for someone else might not work for you. The key is to understand the basic principles and then apply them to your unique situation.

Now, let's talk about a concept that's crucial for reaching major financial goals: the "Opportunity Fund." This is separate from your emergency fund and your retirement savings. It's money you set aside for big goals or experiences – maybe a dream vacation, a down payment on a house, or starting your own business.

The Opportunity Fund is your "yes" fund. It allows you to say yes to life's big opportunities without derailing your long-term financial plans or going into debt. It's the financial equivalent of having your cake and eating it too. To build your Opportunity Fund, start by identifying your big goals. Then, just like with your emergency fund and retirement savings, automate contributions to this fund. Even small, regular contributions can add up over time.

The goal isn't to live like a miser now so you can be rich later. It's about finding a balance that allows you to enjoy life now while also building for the future.

One of the biggest challenges in building your financial fortress is staying motivated over the long haul. It's easy to get excited about saving and investing at first, but it can be hard to maintain that enthusiasm when progress seems slow.

This is where setting clear, specific goals can be incredibly helpful. Instead of a vague goal like "save more money," try something specific like "save $5,000 for a down payment on a house by December 31st." This gives you a clear target to aim for and a deadline to motivate you.

It can also be helpful to visualize your goals. If you're saving for a house, keep a picture of your dream home as your phone wallpaper. If you're saving for retirement, try using one of those age-progression apps to see what you might look like in your golden years. It might sound silly, but research has shown that being able to visualize our future selves can make us more likely to save for the future.

Another powerful motivator is tracking your progress. There's something incredibly satisfying about watching your savings grow or seeing your net worth increase over time. Many banks and investment platforms offer tools to help you track your progress, or you can use a spreadsheet if you prefer.

Building a financial fortress is a marathon, not a sprint. There will be setbacks along the way. The stock market will have bad years. Unexpected expenses will crop up. The key is to stay focused on your long-term goals and keep moving forward, even if it's just a little bit at a time.

And don't forget to celebrate your wins, no matter how small.

Did you stick to your budget this month? Celebrate! Did you increase your 401(k) contribution? That deserves a pat on the back.

Building a solid financial foundation isn't easy, and you deserve credit for every step in the right direction.

In the end, building your financial fortress is about more than just money. It involves creating security, reducing stress, and giving yourself the freedom to live life on your own terms. It's about being able to weather life's storms and take advantage of it's opportunities.

And that, my friends, is worth far more than any number in a bank account.

Key Takeaways:

- Start with an emergency fund of 3-6 months of expenses
- Automate your savings to make it efficient
- Invest for the long term in low-cost, diversified index funds
- Balance saving for the future with enjoying life now
- Use the "Opportunity Fund" concept for major financial goals
- Start investing early to harness the power of compound returns
- Address high-interest debt before focusing on investing
- Set specific, visualizable financial goals to stay motivated
- Track your progress and celebrate your financial wins
- Remember that building a financial fortress is a marathon, not a sprint

PHILIP PETERSON

CHAPTER 9: NAVIGATING LIFE'S FINANCIAL CURVEBALLS

Life has a funny way of throwing financial curveballs when you least expect them. One minute you're cruising along, budget in hand, feeling like a financial wizard. The next, you're staring at an unexpected car repair bill that's about as welcome as a root canal without anesthesia.

Financial curveballs come in all shapes and sizes. They can be as mundane as a broken washing machine or as life-altering as a sudden job loss. Whatever form they take, these unexpected expenses have a knack for derailing even the most carefully laid financial plans.

The average American faces about $2,000 in unexpected expenses each year. That's like being told you have to buy a new iPhone every single year, whether you want to or not. And let's face it, most of us aren't exactly rolling in spare cash.

But here's what's interesting: while we can't predict when these financial surprises will pop up, we can prepare for them. It's like carrying an umbrella - you might not need it every day, but when it rains, you'll be damn glad you have it.

In this chapter, we're going to dive into the art of financial flexibility. We'll explore how to create a budget that bends without breaking, prepare for major life events without going broke, and develop strategies to weather unexpected storms like job loss or income reduction. Think of it as your personal financial storm shelter.

The Flexible Budget: Your Financial Yoga Practice

Creating a flexible budget is a lot like practicing yoga. It's all about balance, strength, and the ability to adapt to changing conditions. Just as a skilled yogi can transition smoothly from one pose to another, a well-designed flexible budget allows you to shift your financial priorities without toppling over.

The first step in creating a flexible budget is to understand your financial foundation. This means getting intimately acquainted with your income, fixed expenses, and discretionary spending. It's like taking inventory of your financial wardrobe - you need to know what you have before you can decide what to wear.

Start by listing all your sources of income. This includes your regular paycheck, any side hustles, investment returns, and that $20 bill your grandma sends you every birthday.

Next, catalog your fixed expenses - these are the non-negotiables like rent, utilities, and loan payments.

Finally, track your discretionary spending for a month. This includes everything from your daily latte habit to your Netflix subscription.

Once you have this financial snapshot, it's time to start building flexibility into your budget. One effective technique is the "50/30/20 rule." This approach suggests allocating 50% of your income to needs, 30% to wants, and 20% to savings and debt repayment. The beauty of this system is it's built-in flexibility. If an unexpected expense crops up, you can temporarily reallocate funds from your "wants" category to cover it.

Another key to a flexible budget is to build in buffer

zones. This means overestimating your expenses slightly and underestimating your income. It's like giving yourself a little financial wiggle room. If you think your grocery bill will be $400 this month, budget $425. If you end up spending less, great! You've got a little extra cushion. If not, you're covered.

Remember to review and adjust your budget regularly. Life changes, and your budget should change with it. Maybe you got a raise (congratulations!), or perhaps you've decided to cut back on eating out. Whatever the change, your budget should reflect it. Think of it as a living document, not something set in stone.

Preparing for Life's Big Moments (Without Breaking the Bank)

Life's major events have a way of sneaking up on us. One day you're single and carefree, the next you're planning a wedding, buying a house, or welcoming a tiny human into the world. These milestones are exciting, but they can also be seriously expensive if you're not prepared.

Let's start with weddings. The average wedding in the U.S. costs around $30,000. That's enough to make anyone consider eloping to Vegas. But with some smart planning, you can have your cake and eat it too (literally - wedding cake is delicious).

Start by setting a realistic budget based on what you can afford, not what the wedding industry tells you you need. A beautiful wedding doesn't have to mean an expensive one. Consider off-peak dates, DIY decorations, and prioritizing what's truly important to you. Maybe you splurge on the photographer but save on flowers by using seasonal blooms.

Next up: buying a house. This is probably the biggest purchase you'll ever make, so it pays to be prepared. Start saving for a down payment as early as possible. Aim for 20% of the home's value to avoid private mortgage insurance. But don't neglect your emergency fund in the process - you don't want to be house-rich and cash-poor.

Research first-time homebuyer programs in your area. Many states offer assistance with down payments or favorable loan terms for first-time buyers. And don't forget to factor in all the hidden costs of homeownership, like property taxes, insurance, and maintenance. Owning a home is great, but it's not so great if you can't afford to fix the roof when it starts leaking.

Now, let's talk about the ultimate budget-buster: having a kid. The USDA estimates that it costs about $233,610 to raise a child from birth to age 17. That's not including college, which is a whole other financial beast. Start preparing financially as soon as you start thinking about having kids. Build up your emergency fund, because trust me, you'll need it. Look into your company's parental leave policy and start budgeting for reduced income if necessary.

Research childcare costs in your area - they can be shockingly high in some places. Consider opening a 529 college savings plan as soon as your little one arrives. These plans offer tax advantages and can help ease the burden of future education costs. And don't forget about life insurance - it's not fun to think about, but it's crucial to protect your family financially.

Key Idea: The "Sinking Fund" Strategy. For major life events, consider setting up "sinking funds." These are separate savings accounts dedicated to specific goals. Set up automatic transfers to these accounts each month. This way, you're consistently saving for big expenses without feeling the pinch all at once.

When Life Gives You Lemons: Handling Job Loss or

Income Reduction

Losing your job or facing a significant income reduction is about as fun as a root canal performed by a blindfolded dentist. But with the right strategies, you can weather this storm and come out stronger on the other side.

First things first: don't panic. I know, easier said than done when your main source of income just disappeared. But panicking leads to rash decisions, and rash decisions rarely lead to good financial outcomes. Instead, take a deep breath and assess your situation. How much do you have in your emergency fund? What are your essential expenses? How long can you cover these expenses with your current savings? This financial triage will help you develop a clear picture of where you stand.

Next, slash your expenses like you're wielding a machete in a jungle of unnecessary costs. Cancel subscriptions, cut back on dining out, and put any non-essential purchases on hold. You'd be surprised how much you can save when you really put your mind to it. Look into unemployment benefits if you've lost your job. The process can be a bit of a bureaucratic maze, but it's worth navigating for the financial lifeline it can provide. Don't let pride get in the way - these benefits exist for exactly this kind of situation.

If you're facing a reduction in income rather than a finish loss, consider picking up a side hustle. The gig economy has made it easier than ever to earn extra cash on the side. Whether it's driving for a rideshare service, freelancing in your field, or selling handmade crafts online, every little bit helps.

Don't neglect your health insurance. If you've lost your job, you may be eligible for COBRA coverage, which allows you to continue your employer-sponsored health insurance for a limited time. It can be expensive, but it's often cheaper than paying for medical care out of pocket if something goes wrong.

This situation is temporary. Use this time to reassess your career goals and potentially pivot to a new field. Take online courses to upgrade your skills. Network like your financial life depends on it (because, well, it kind of does).

The Crisis-Proof Budget: Building Financial Resilience

Creating a crisis-proof budget is like building a financial fortress. It's about constructing strong walls to protect you from external threats while maintaining the flexibility to adapt to changing conditions. The foundation of a crisis-proof budget is a robust emergency fund. Aim to save 3-6 months of living expenses in a easily accessible savings account. This might seem like a lot, but trust me, when a crisis hits, you'll be glad you have it.

Next, diversify your income streams. This could mean starting a side business, investing in dividend-paying stocks, or developing passive income sources like rental properties. The goal is to avoid relying on a single source of income. It's the financial equivalent of not putting all your eggs in one basket.

Automate your savings and bill payments. This confirms that you're consistently saving and meeting your financial obligations, even if life gets hectic. Set up automatic transfers to your savings accounts and use auto-pay for your bills. It's like putting your finances on autopilot.

Regularly review and update your insurance coverage. This includes health insurance, life insurance, and property insurance. Adequate coverage can protect you from financial catastrophe in case of unexpected events.

Develop your skills and keep your resume updated. Your skills are your most valuable asset in the job market. Continuously improving them makes you more resilient to job loss or industry changes.

Finally, practice living below your means. This doesn't mean living like a monk, but rather being intentional about your spending and prioritizing what truly matters to you. It revolves around creating a gap between your income and your expenses, which gives you more financial flexibility.

Learning from Financial Setbacks: Turning Lemons into Lemonade

Financial setbacks are never fun, but they can be incredibly valuable learning experiences if you approach them with the right mindset. It's like falling off a bike - it hurts, but it teaches you how to ride better.

Start by analyzing what went wrong. Was it an unexpected expense you hadn't planned for? Did you underestimate your spending in a certain category? Understanding the root cause can help you prevent similar issues in the future.

Use setbacks as motivation to improve your financial literacy. Read books, take online courses, or talk to a financial advisor. The more you know about managing money, the better equipped you'll be to handle future challenges.

Adjust your budget based on what you've learned. Maybe you need to allocate more to your emergency fund or cut back in certain areas. Use the setback as a catalyst for positive change in your financial habits. Don't be too hard on yourself. Financial setbacks happen to everyone, even the most financially savvy among us. What matters is how you respond and what you learn from the experience.

Interesting Fact: *The Importance of Financial Resilience. Studies have shown that financially resilient individuals weather economic storms better and report higher levels of overall life satisfaction. It's not about how much money you have, but how well you manage what you* **have.**

Problems to Watch Out For: The Financial Landmines

Even with the best planning, there are some common pitfalls, problems, issues, problems, issues that can derail your financial resilience. Being aware of these can help you avoid them.

One major pitfall, problem, issue, problem, issue is lifestyle inflation. As your income increases, it's tempting to upgrade your lifestyle accordingly. But maintaining your current lifestyle and saving the difference can significantly boost your financial resilience.

Another common mistake is neglecting to update your budget as your life changes. Your budget should evolve with you. A budget that worked when you were single might not cut it when you're married with kids. Avoid the temptation to use credit cards to cover unexpected expenses. While it might seem like a quick fix, it can lead to a cycle of debt that's hard to break. This is where your emergency fund comes in handy.

Don't make emotional financial decisions. Whether it's panic-selling investments during a market downturn or making a large impulse purchase, emotions and finances rarely mix well. Take a step back and think critically before making significant financial moves.

Beware of the "it won't happen to me" mentality. Many people underestimate the likelihood of financial emergencies, leading to inadequate preparation. Always hope for the best, but plan for the worst.

Adapting Your Financial Strategy: One Size Doesn't Fit All

While the principles of financial resilience are universal, how you apply them may vary depending on your specific situation. Here are some tips for adapting your strategy to different scenarios:

For freelancers or gig workers with irregular income, consider using the "pay yourself first" method. Set aside a percentage of each paycheck for savings before allocating the rest to expenses. This confirms you're always saving, even when income fluctuates. If you're in a high-cost-of-living area, you might need to allocate a larger percentage of your income to housing. In this case, look for creative ways to cut costs in other areas or consider ways to increase your income.

For those with student loans or other significant debt, focus on creating a debt repayment strategy alongside building your emergency fund. The debt avalanche method (paying off highest interest debt first) can be particularly effective.

If you're caring for aging parents or have other family obligations, factor these potential costs into your financial planning. Consider long-term care insurance or setting up a separate savings fund for family care. For those nearing retirement, your crisis-proof budget might include a larger cash cushion and a more conservative investment mix to protect against market downturns.

The key is to tailor these strategies to your unique circumstances while still adhering to the core principles of financial resilience.

Key Takeaways:

- Create a flexible budget that allows for adjustments when life throws curveballs
- Build a robust emergency fund covering 3-6 months of expenses
- Prepare for major life events by setting up sinking funds and researching costs in advance
- Diversify your income streams to reduce reliance on a single source
- Regularly review and update your budget, insurance coverage, and financial goals
- Learn from financial setbacks and use them as opportunities for growth
- Avoid common pitfalls, problems, issues, problems, issues like lifestyle inflation and emotional financial decisions
- Adapt your financial strategy to your unique circumstances while maintaining core principles of resilience
- Automate savings and bill payments to confirm consistent financial habits
- Continuously educate yourself about personal finance to make informed decisions

CHAPTER 10: THE FAMILY FINANCE FACTOR - BUDGETING AS A TEAM

Money talks, but in most families, it's usually shouting. I've seen couples who can agree on everything from politics to pizza toppings suddenly transform into snarling beasts when the topic of finances rears it's ugly head. It's as if the mere mention of a budget causes a temporary form of insanity, turning otherwise rational adults into squabbling toddlers fighting over the last cookie.

But here's what's interesting: family budgeting doesn't have to be a battleground. In fact, when done right, it can be the glue that holds a household together, creating a shared sense of purpose and achievement. It's like a financial group hug, only with spreadsheets and fewer awkward moments.

Money management as a family unit is a relatively modern concept. Back in the 18th century, it was primarily the domain of women to keep the household books. Men were too busy being important and growing impressive sideburns to bother with such trivial matters.

Fast forward to today, and we're still figuring out how to navigate these financial waters together without capsizing the family boat. Don't worry, I've brought floaties.

The Great Money Merger

Merging finances without merging frustrations is about as easy as herding cats while blindfolded. But don't worry, it's not impossible. The key is communication, and lots of it. You need to talk about money more than you talk about what to watch on

Netflix, and that's saying something.

Start by laying all your financial cards on the table. And I mean all of them - credit card statements, bank accounts, that secret stash of quarters you've been hoarding since college. Everything.

This isn't the time for financial skeletons in the closet. Trust me, they have a nasty habit of falling out at the worst possible moment, usually when you're trying to impress the in-laws or buy a house. Once everything's out in the open, it's time to have The Talk. No, not that talk.

The money talk. Discuss your financial goals, your spending habits, and your deepest, darkest money fears. Do you wake up in a cold sweat thinking about retirement? Does the thought of your partner's shoe collection make you want to hide the credit cards? Get it all out there.

Now, here's where it gets tricky. You need to find a system that works for both of you. Some couples swear by joint accounts, others prefer to keep things separate with a joint account for shared expenses. There's no one-size-fits-all solution here. It's like choosing between boxers and briefs - it's a personal preference, and what works for one couple might be incredibly uncomfortable for another.

The Budget Balancing Act

Creating a unified family financial vision is like trying to get everyone to agree on where to go for dinner - it requires diplomacy, compromise, and occasionally, bribery. (I'm kidding about the bribery. Mostly.)

Start by setting some shared goals. Maybe you want to save for a family vacation, or perhaps you're aiming to pay off that mountain of credit card debt that's been looming over you like a disapproving mother-in-law. Whatever it is, make sure everyone's on board.

Next, track your spending. And I mean really track it. Every coffee, every impulse buy, every "it was on sale" purchase. You might be surprised (or horrified) to uncover where your money's actually going. I once tracked my spending and realized I was spending more on fancy coffee each month than on my electricity bill.

Needless to say, I invested in a good home coffee maker after that revelation. Once you know where your money's going, it's time to allocate it. The 50/30/20 rule is a good starting point - 50% for needs, 30% for wants, and 20% for savings and debt repayment.

But remember, this is a guideline, not a commandment carved in stone. Adjust as needed to fit your family's unique situation.

The Kids Are Alright (Or Will Be, Once They Learn About Money)

Teaching children about budgeting and financial responsibility is crucial, unless you want them living in your basement until they're 40, subsisting on a diet of ramen noodles and broken dreams.

Start early. As soon as they can count, they can start learning about money. Use piggy banks, create simple budgets for their allowance, and explain the basics of saving and spending.

And for the love of all that is holy, teach them the difference between needs and wants. No, little Timmy, a new Xbox is not a need, no matter how convincingly you argue.

As they get older, involve them in family financial discussions. Let them see how you budget, how you make financial decisions, and yes, even how you sometimes make mistakes. It's better they learn from your errors than repeat them on their own. Consider giving them real-world experience. When my daughter wanted a new bike, we set up a savings plan.

She had to save half the cost from her allowance and odd jobs, and we matched the other half. It took her six months, but she learned valuable lessons about delayed gratification and the value of money.

Key Idea: *The Family Financial Roundtable. Regular family meetings where all members, including children, join in budget discussions can foster transparency, teach financial responsibility, and confirm everyone's voice is heard in financial decisions.*

When Money Talks, Listen (But Don't Shout)

Handling financial disagreements constructively is about as easy as performing brain surgery while riding a unicycle. But it's a skill worth mastering unless you want every discussion about money to end in slammed doors and silent treatments.

First, remember that you're on the same team. It's not you versus your partner, it's both of you versus the problem. Approach disagreements with a collaborative mindset, not a combative one.

Second, listen. Really listen. Not the kind of listening where you're just waiting for your turn to speak, but active, engaged listening. Try to understand your partner's perspective, even if you don't agree with it.

Third, focus on solutions, not blame. It doesn't matter whose fault it is that you're in this financial pickle. What matters is how you're going to get out of it. Together.

And finally, if things get heated, take a break. Money discussions can be emotional, and sometimes you need to step away and cool off. It's better to pause and come back later than to say something you'll regret.

The Budget Busters

Even the best-laid budget plans can go awry. Life has a funny way of throwing financial curveballs when you least expect them. The car breaks down, the roof starts leaking, or your kid suddenly decides they need braces and a new wardrobe on the same day.

The key to handling these budget busters is to expect the unexpected. Build an emergency fund into your budget. Aim for 3-6 months of living expenses tucked away in a easily accessible savings account. It's like a financial security blanket, only less fuzzy and more practical.

Also, be flexible. Your budget shouldn't be set in stone. Review it regularly and be prepared to adjust as circumstances change. Maybe you got a raise (congratulations!), or maybe your utility bills have gone up (my condolences). Whatever the case, your budget should evolve with your life.

The Digital Divide

In this age of apps and algorithms, there's no shortage of digital tools to help with family budgeting. From Mint to YNAB (You Need A Budget), there's an app for every budgeting style and preference.

But, the best budgeting tool is the one you'll actually use. It doesn't matter if it's a state-of-the-art app or a pen and paper ledger like your great-grandma used. What matters is that it works for you and your family.

Personally, I'm a fan of the digital approach. It's easier to track spending when every transaction is automatically categorized and you can see pretty graphs of where your money's going. Plus, it's harder to "forget" about that impulse purchase when it's staring you in the face every time you open the app.

But if you're more of an analog person, that's fine too. The important thing is consistency. Whatever method you choose, stick with it.

The Long Game

Budgeting for long-term goals like education or retirement can feel like trying to fill an Olympic-sized swimming pool with a teaspoon. It's daunting, it's time-consuming, and sometimes you wonder if you're making any progress at all. But here's the secret: it's not about big, dramatic gestures. It's about consistent, small actions over time.

That $5 you save by skipping your daily latte? If invested wisely, it could grow to a tidy sum by the time your toddler is ready for college.

Start by setting clear, specific long-term goals. Don't just say "save for retirement." Say "save $1 million for retirement by age 65." It's specific, it's measurable, and it gives you something concrete to work towards.

Then, break that big goal down into smaller, manageable chunks. How much do you need to save each year? Each month? Each paycheck? Suddenly, that enormous goal doesn't seem quite so insurmountable.

And remember, it's never too early to start. The power of compound interest is like a financial superpower. The earlier you start saving and investing, the less you actually have to save to reach your goals. It's like magic, only better because it's real.

Interesting Fact: The concept of 'pay yourself first' in budgeting was introduced by George Clason in his 1926 book 'The Richest Man in Babylon.' This principle suggests setting aside a portion of your income for savings before budgeting for expenses.

The Spender and the Saver: A Financial Romeo and Juliet

It's a tale as old as time: one partner is a spender, the other a saver. One sees money as a tool for enjoyment, the other as a shield against future hardships. It's like a financial version of "The Odd Couple," only with higher stakes and less laugh track.

If this sounds familiar, don't panic. Opposites can attract, even when it comes to money management. The key is to find a middle ground that respects both perspectives.

Start by acknowledging the strengths of each approach. The spender might be great at finding joy in the present and seizing opportunities. The saver might excel at providing security and planning for the future. Both are valuable skills.

Then, work on compromises. Maybe the saver agrees to a "fun money" category in the budget, while the spender commits to automatic savings contributions. It's about finding a balance that allows both partners to feel comfortable and respected.

Your differences can be a strength if you let them. The spender can help the saver learn to enjoy life more in the present, while the saver can help provide a sense of security and future planning. It's a financial yin and yang.

The Communication Conundrum

Effective communication about money is about as natural for most couples as doing the cha-cha in scuba gear. It's awkward, it's uncomfortable, and there's a good chance someone's going to step on someone else's toes.

But, good financial communication is the foundation of a healthy family budget. Without it, you're just two people throwing money into a shared pot and hoping for the best.

Set regular "money dates" with your partner. These are dedicated times to discuss your finances, free from distractions. No kids, no TV, no scrolling through your phone. Just you, your partner, and your financial goals.

During these meetings, be honest about your concerns and aspirations. If you're worried about overspending, say so. If you have a dream of starting a business, share it. The more open you are, the easier it becomes to work together towards common goals.

And remember, there's more to it than just the numbers. Discuss your emotions around money too. Are you feeling stressed? Anxious? Excited? Understanding each other's emotional relationship with money can help prevent misunderstandings and conflicts down the road.

Key Takeaways:

- Open communication is the cornerstone of successful family budgeting. Talk early, talk often, and be honest.
- Involve the whole family in the budgeting process, including children. It's never too early to start learning about financial responsibility.
- Set clear, specific financial goals as a family and work together to achieve them.
- Be flexible. Your budget should evolve as your life circumstances change.
- Expect the unexpected. Build an emergency fund into your budget.
- Find a budgeting method that works for your family and stick with it consistently.
- You're on the same team. Approach financial disagreements with a collaborative mindset.
- Balance short-term enjoyment with long-term security. It's okay to have fun with money, as long as you're also planning for the future.
- Regular financial check-ins can help keep you on track and prevent small issues from becoming big problems.
- Celebrate your financial wins together, no matter how small. It helps maintain motivation and makes budgeting feel less like a chore.

CHAPTER 11: THE LONG GAME - BUDGETING FOR FUTURE YOU

Ah, the future. That mystical realm where our dreams of sipping piña coladas on a beach somehow coexist with the nagging fear of eating cat food in our twilight years. It's a peculiar balancing act, isn't it? We're constantly told to live in the moment, and to plan for a future that seems as distant and hazy as a mirage in the Sahara.

I'll admit, I've had my fair share of financial faux pas. There was the time I convinced myself that investing in a friend's artisanal pickle business was a surefire path to riches. Spoiler alert: it wasn't. But through the sour taste of failure (and overpriced cucumbers), I learned a valuable lesson about the importance of long-term financial planning.

Budgeting for your future self is less about crystal ball gazing and more about creating a flexible framework that can adapt to life's inevitable curveballs. It's about striking that delicate balance between enjoying your present life and ensuring that your future self doesn't curse your name every time they open their wallet.

So, let's set off on this pathway of financial time travel together. We'll explore the art and science of long-term budgeting, unravel the mysteries of compound interest, and maybe even figure out how to make our money work harder than we do.

The cornerstone of any long-term financial plan is understanding the power of compound interest. It's a concept so potent that Albert Einstein allegedly called it the "eighth wonder of the world." Now, I'm not one to argue with Einstein, but I'd wager he never had to explain compound interest to a room full of glazed-over eyes at a family dinner.

Here's the gist: compound interest is interest on interest. It's like a snowball rolling down a hill, gathering more snow (or in this case, money) as it goes. The earlier you start, the bigger your snowball gets.

Let's say you invest $1,000 at age 20 with an 8% annual return. By the time you're 65, that $1,000 will have grown to over $30,000. Start at 30, and you're looking at about $14,000. The moral of the story? Time is literally money.

But compound interest isn't about watching your money grow while you twiddle your thumbs. It's about making strategic decisions now that will pay off exponentially in the future. This might mean foregoing that daily latte (I know, I know, personal finance advice and lattes are a cliché, but bear with me) and investing the difference. It revolves around understanding that small sacrifices now can lead to significant gains later.

Now, let's talk about the elephant in the room: retirement. For many of us, the word conjures images of gray-haired guys playing shuffleboard on a cruise ship.
But retirement planning is about so much more than ensuring you have enough money for tacky Hawaiian shirts and early bird specials.

The first step in retirement planning is figuring out how much you'll need. A common rule of thumb is the 4% rule, which suggests you can withdraw 4% of your retirement savings each year without running out of money. So, if you want an annual income of $40,000 in retirement, you'd need a nest egg of about $1 million. I know, I just heard your jaw hit the floor from here.

But before you resign yourself to a future of working until

you're 105, remember that this is just a guideline. Your actual needs will depend on a variety of factors, including your lifestyle, health, and whether you plan to spend your golden years backpacking across Europe or puttering around in your garden.

One of the most effective ways to save for retirement is through tax-advantaged accounts like 401(k)s and IRAs. These accounts allow your money to grow tax-free or tax-deferred, giving compound interest an even bigger boost. If your employer offers a 401(k) match, that's essentially free money. Not taking advantage of it is like leaving a pile of cash on the sidewalk and walking away.

But retirement isn't the only long-term goal you should be budgeting for. Life has a funny way of throwing expensive curveballs our way.

Maybe you dream of buying a house, starting a business, or funding your child's education. Each of these goals requires it's own savings strategy.

For shorter-term goals (think 5-10 years), you might want to consider more conservative investments like high-yield savings accounts or certificates of deposit. For longer-term goals, you can afford to take on more risk with stock market investments, giving your money more time to weather market ups and downs.

One often overlooked aspect of long-term budgeting is planning for major life transitions. Career changes, for instance, can have a significant impact on your financial trajectory. Maybe you've always dreamed of ditching your corporate job to become a yoga instructor. Noble as that may be, it's probably going to come with a pay cut. Planning for these transitions means building up a substantial emergency fund and possibly even a "career transition" fund.

Early retirement is another transition that requires careful planning. The FIRE (Financial Independence, Retire Early) movement has gained traction in recent years, with proponents aiming to retire in their 30s or 40s.

While the idea of telling your boss to take this job and shove it at 35 might be appealing, it requires an intense level of saving and investing. We're talking saving 50-70% of your income. It's not for the faint of heart, but for those who can pull it off, it can lead to a life of freedom and flexibility.

Key Insight: *The concept of "retirement" is evolving. For many, it's less about stopping work entirely and more about achieving financial independence - the ability to work (or not) on your own terms.*

Now, let's talk about the elephant in the room that nobody wants to discuss: healthcare costs. In the U.S., healthcare is one of the biggest expenses in retirement, with some estimates suggesting that a 65-year-old couple might need $300,000 saved just for medical expenses. It's enough to make you want to start stockpiling vitamins and bubble wrap.

Planning for these costs means understanding your insurance options. Medicare is available starting at age 65, but it doesn't cover everything. Long-term care insurance is another option to consider, though it can be expensive. The key is to start thinking about these costs early and factor them into your long-term budget.

Insurance, in general, plays a crucial role in long-term financial planning. Life insurance, for instance, can provide a safety net for your loved ones if something happens to you. Disability insurance protects your income if you're unable to work. These policies are like financial umbrellas - you hope you never need them, but you're glad to have them when it starts pouring.

Another aspect of long-term budgeting that often gets overlooked is estate planning. Now, I know what you're thinking - "Estate planning? I barely have two nickels to rub together, let alone an estate!" But estate planning isn't just for the wealthy. It's about ensuring your wishes are carried out and your loved ones are taken care of after you're gone.

This brings us to the concept of legacy planning. It's not just about passing on money, and about passing on values and financial education to future generations. Teaching your children about budgeting, saving, and investing can be one of the most valuable gifts you can give them.

So, how do we tie all of this together into a cohesive long-term budgeting strategy? Here's a step-by-step approach:

1. **Define your long-term goals:** Retirement, home ownership, starting a business - whatever they may be, get clear on what you're working towards.
2. **Assess your current financial situation:** Take stock of your income, expenses, assets, and debts.
3. **Calculate the gap:** Figure out how much you need to save to reach your goals.
4. **Create a budget that prioritizes saving:** Pay yourself first by automating transfers to your savings and investment accounts.
5. **Invest wisely:** Understand your risk tolerance and invest accordingly. Time in the market beats timing the market.
6. **Protect your downside:** Ensure you have adequate insurance coverage and an emergency fund.
7. **Review and adjust regularly:** Life changes, and your financial plan should change with it. Review your plan at least annually.

8. **Plan for the unexpected:** Build flexibility into your plan to account for life's curveballs.
9. **Think beyond yourself:** Consider how your financial decisions impact your family and future generations.

Important Tip: Automate your savings and investments. Set up automatic transfers to your savings and investment accounts on payday. What you don't see, you won't miss.

Now, let's address some common pitfalls, problems, issues, problems, issues in long-term budgeting. One of the biggest is underestimating inflation. That $1 million nest egg might sound impressive now, but in 30 years, it might have the purchasing power of a ham sandwich. When budgeting for the future, always factor in inflation.

Another common mistake is failing to diversify. Putting all your eggs in one basket is risky, whether that basket is real estate, stocks, or your company's stock options. A well-diversified portfolio can help protect you from market volatility and economic downturns.

Emotional decision-making is another pitfall, problem, issue, problem, issue to avoid. It's easy to panic when the stock market takes a nosedive or get caught up in the hype of the latest investment fad (I'm looking at you, crypto millionaires). But successful long-term investing requires a cool head and a steady hand. Stick to your plan, and don't let short-term market movements derail your long-term goals.

Lastly, don't forget to enjoy the present while planning for the future. I've seen too many people become so focused on saving for tomorrow that they forget to live for today. Life is short, and while it's important to plan for the future, it's equally important to enjoy the journey. Find a balance that allows you to save for your goals while still enjoying life's little pleasures.

The goal of long-term budgeting isn't to become the richest person in the graveyard. It revolves around creating a life of financial security and freedom, both now and in the future. It's about having the means to pursue your passions, take care of your loved ones, and leave a positive impact on the world.

So, as you set off on your long-term budgeting journey, keep your eyes on the horizon but don't forget to enjoy the view along the way.

Key Takeaways

- Start early: The power of compound interest is on your side.
- Define clear, specific long-term goals.
- Create a budget that prioritizes saving and investing.
- Diversify your investments to manage risk.
- Plan for major life transitions and unexpected events.
- Factor in healthcare costs and insurance needs.
- Regularly review and adjust your plan.
- Educate yourself and stay informed about financial matters.
- Balance saving for the future with enjoying the present.
- Consider the impact of your financial decisions on future generations.

CHAPTER 12: TECH-SAVVY BUDGETING - LEVERAGING DIGITAL TOOLS FOR FINANCIAL SUCCESS

Digital tools have revolutionized personal finance management in ways that would make our grandparents' heads spin. Remember those clunky old checkbook registers? They're about as relevant now as a horse-drawn carriage in rush hour traffic.

Today's budgeting apps are like having a team of accountants, financial advisors, and fortune tellers right in your pocket. They crunch numbers faster than you can say "compound interest" and spit out predictions about your financial future that would make Nostradamus jealous.

But let's not get ahead of ourselves. The journey from pen-and-paper ledgers to AI-powered financial assistants has been a wild ride. It all started back in the 1980s when some clever clogs decided to merge personal computers with money management.

Software like Managing Your Money and Quicken, which were about as user-friendly as a brick wall but still managed to capture the imagination of tech-savvy penny-pinchers everywhere. Fast forward a few decades, and we've got smartphones that can track every penny we spend, invest, or lose down the back of the sofa. The global personal finance software market is expected to hit a whopping $1.5 billion by 2027. That's a lot of digital piggy banks.

But here's what's interesting: despite all this whiz-bang technology, many of us are still about as good at managing our money as a toddler in a candy store. It's not for lack of tools, mind you. We're drowning in apps that promise to turn us into the next Warren Buffett. The problem is knowing which ones to use and how to use them effectively.

We'll look at everything from the cream of the crop in budgeting apps to the brave new world of AI-powered predictive budgeting. We'll even tackle the thorny issue of cybersecurity because let's face it, the last thing you want is some spotty teenager in a basement halfway around the world getting their grubby mitts on your hard-earned cash.

First up, let's talk about the crème de la crème of budgeting apps. These digital marvels come in all shapes and sizes, from the sleek and simple to the complex and feature-packed.

At the top of the heap, you've got apps like Mint, YNAB (You Need A Budget), and Personal Capital. Each has it's own unique flavor, like financial ice cream for your smartphone.

Mint, for instance, is the Swiss Army knife of budgeting apps. It does everything short of making you a cup of coffee in the morning.

It syncs with your bank accounts, credit cards, and investment portfolios faster than you can say "where did all my money go?" It categorizes your spending automatically, sets up budgets, and even wags it's digital finger at you when you overspend. It's like having a financially savvy parent living in your phone, minus the guilt trips about not calling often enough.

YNAB, on the other hand, is for those who like to get their hands dirty with their finances. It's based on the zero-based budgeting method, which is a fancy way of saying "give every dollar a job." Using YNAB is like being the CEO of your own personal economy. You assign roles to your money, telling it where to go and what to do. It's perfect for control freaks and those who find spreadsheets sexier than a romance novel.

Then there's Personal Capital, the sophisticated cousin of the budgeting app world. While it does offer budgeting features, it's real strength comes from investment tracking and management. It's like having a robot financial advisor that never sleeps, constantly analyzing your portfolio and offering suggestions. If Mint is a Honda Civic (reliable and gets the job done), Personal Capital is a Tesla (flashy, high-tech, and makes you feel like you're living in the future).

But these are just the tip of the iceberg. There are more budgeting apps out there than flavors of potato chips, each with it's own unique features.

Some, like Goodbudget, use the envelope method digitally, allowing you to divide your money into virtual envelopes for different expenses. Others, like Clarity Money, use AI to analyze your spending habits and find ways to save you money, like a digital bloodhound sniffing out savings.

The beauty of these apps is that they take the drudgery out of budgeting. No more spending hours hunched over a calculator, trying to figure out where all your money went. These apps do the heavy lifting for you, giving you a clear picture of your finances faster than you can say "avocado toast."

But here's where it gets really interesting. We're not just talking about apps that track your spending. Oh no, we're in the age of predictive budgeting, where AI and machine learning are joining forces to become your personal financial fortune teller.

Imagine an app that doesn't just tell you where your money went, but where it's likely to go in the future. These AI-powered tools analyze your spending patterns, factor in variables like seasonal expenses and upcoming bills, and then predict your future financial state with scary accuracy. It's like having a crystal ball, but instead of vague prophecies about tall, dark strangers, you get specific forecasts about your bank balance.

Some of these predictive tools can even factor in external data, like economic trends or changes in your industry, to give you a heads up about potential financial bumps in the road. It's like having a financial weather forecast: "Cloudy with a chance of unexpected expenses."

But as with any technology, there's a flip side to this coin (pun absolutely intended). While these apps can be incredibly useful, they also raise some thorny questions about privacy and security.

Key Insight: While AI-powered budgeting tools offer unprecedented insights into your financial future, it's crucial to understand their limitations. They're based on historical data and patterns, which means they can't account for unexpected life changes or economic shifts. Use them as a guide, not a gospel.

Now, let's talk about the elephant in the room: cybersecurity. In an age where hackers seem to be always one step ahead, how safe is it to put all your financial data into an app? It's a valid concern, and one that keeps many people clinging to their paper ledgers like a life raft in a digital sea.

Most reputable budgeting apps use bank-level encryption to protect your data. They're often more secure than your average website, employing many layers of protection to keep the bad guys out. But that doesn't mean you can just download any old app and start punching in your bank details willy-nilly.

When choosing a budgeting app, look for ones that use two-factor authentication, encrypt data both in transit and at rest, and have a solid track record when it comes to security. It's also a good idea to check if they're regulated by financial authorities.

For instance, in the US, many fintech companies are overseen by the Financial Industry Regulatory Authority (FINRA). But even with all these safeguards, the weakest link in your financial security is often... well, you. Using "password123" as your password is like leaving your front door wide open with a sign saying "Burglars Welcome." Use strong, unique passwords for each of your financial apps, enable two-factor authentication wherever possible, and for the love of all that is holy, don't access your financial apps on public Wi-Fi networks.

Now, let's shift gears and talk about a trend that's been gaining momentum: cashless budgeting. With the rise of contactless payments, digital wallets, and cryptocurrency, cold hard cash is becoming about as common as a phone booth. This shift has some interesting implications for budgeting.

On the plus side, going cashless makes tracking your spending a breeze. Every transaction is recorded digitally, which means no more trying to remember where that missing $20 went. It's all there in black and white (or whatever color scheme your budgeting app uses).

Cashless budgeting also makes it easier to automate your finances. You can set up automatic transfers to your savings account, schedule bill payments, and even round up your purchases to the nearest dollar and invest the difference. It's like having a robot assistant managing your money for you.

But there's a potential downside to this frictionless spending. When you're not physically handing over cash, it's easy to lose touch with how much you're actually spending. There's a psychological aspect to parting with physical money that doesn't quite translate to tapping a card or waving your phone. It's like the difference between eating a whole cake and just licking the frosting - one feels a lot more substantial than the other.

Some budgeting apps are trying to bridge this gap by providing visual representations of your spending. They might show your budget as a series of jars that empty as you spend, or use color-coding to indicate when you're approaching your limits. It's an try to recreate that tangible feeling of watching your money dwindle, without the need to carry around a wad of cash.

Important Tip: *If you're struggling with overspending in a cashless world, try using the "envelope method" digitally. Allocate specific amounts to different spending categories at the start of each month, and once a category is empty, that's it - no more spending in that area until next month. It's like having digital willpower.*

As we peer into the crystal ball of fintech, some exciting trends are emerging that could change the face of personal finance management. One of the most intriguing is the integration of augmented reality (AR) into budgeting apps.

Imagine pointing your phone camera at a product in a store and instantly seeing how it fits into your budget, complete with a 3D visualization of it's impact on your financial goals. Or picture a virtual financial advisor appearing in your living room, walking you through complex investment decisions with interactive charts and graphs floating in the air. It sounds like something out of a sci-fi movie, but it's closer to reality than you might think.

Another trend to watch is the rise of voice-activated financial assistants. We're already used to asking Alexa or Siri for the weather forecast or to play our favorite songs. Soon, we might be saying things like, "Hey Google, how much do I have left in my dining out budget this month?" or "Siri, transfer $100 to my savings account." It's the ultimate in hands-free money management.

But perhaps the most significant trend is the move towards open banking. This is the practice of banks sharing your financial data (with your permission, of course) with third-party providers. It sounds scary, but it has the potential to alter personal finance management.

With open banking, your budgeting app could have real-time access to all your financial accounts, not just the ones you've manually linked. This means more accurate budgeting, better financial insights, and the ability to switch between financial products more easily. It's like giving your budgeting app x-ray vision into your finances.

Of course, with great power comes great responsibility. As these technologies evolve, so too must our approach to financial literacy and digital security. It's not enough to just download an app and hope for the best.

We need to understand how these tools work, what they're capable of, and how to use them effectively and safely.

So, how do you go about implementing all this tech-savvy budgeting goodness into your life? Here's a step-by-step guide to get you started:

1. Assess your current financial situation. What are your income sources? What are your regular expenses? What are your financial goals?
2. Research and choose your tools. Based on your needs and goals, choose a budgeting app that fits your style. The best app is the one you'll actually use consistently.
3. Link your accounts. Most budgeting apps work best when they have a complete picture of your finances. Link all your bank accounts, credit cards, and investment accounts.

4. Categorize your expenses. While many apps do this automatically, you'll likely need to do some manual categorization at first to ensure accuracy.
5. Set up your budget. Use the insights from your expense tracking to create realistic budget categories. Don't forget to include savings goals!
6. Enable notifications. Let your app remind you when bills are due, when you're approaching budget limits, or when it spots unusual spending patterns.
7. Review and adjust regularly. Your budget isn't set in stone. Review it monthly and make adjustments as your financial situation and goals change.
8. Explore advanced features. Once you're comfortable with the basics, start exploring features like investment tracking, debt payoff strategies, or predictive budgeting.
9. Stay secure. Regularly update your app, use strong passwords, and enable two-factor authentication. Be cautious about accessing financial information on public Wi-Fi networks.
10. Keep learning. Stay informed about new features and tools that could help you manage your money even more effectively.

The goal of all this tech wizardry isn't to make budgeting more complicated. It's to make it easier, more accurate, and dare I say, even a bit fun. (Okay, maybe "fun" is stretching it, but certainly less painful than trying to balance a checkbook by hand.)

The bottom line is this: technology has given us unprecedented control over our finances. We have tools at our fingertips that our parents and grandparents could only dream of. But like any tool, their effectiveness depends on how we use them. A budgeting app can't force you to stop buying overpriced lattes or impulse-purchasing gadgets you don't need. It can, however, make you acutely aware of how those decisions impact your overall financial health.

In the end, tech-savvy budgeting is about using technology to make informed decisions about your money. It's about harnessing the power of data and automation to build a solid financial foundation. And who knows?

With these tools in your arsenal, you might just find yourself on the path to becoming the next Warren Buffett. Or at the very least, someone who doesn't break into a cold sweat when checking their bank balance.

Key Takeaways

- Digital budgeting tools have evolved from simple software to AI-powered financial assistants.
- Top budgeting apps like Mint, YNAB, and Personal Capital offer unique features to suit different financial management styles.
- AI and machine learning enable predictive budgeting, offering insights into future financial states.
- Cybersecurity is crucial when using digital financial tools. Look for apps with strong security measures and practice good digital hygiene.
- Cashless budgeting offers convenience but may disconnect users from their spending. Visual representations in apps can help bridge this gap.
- Emerging trends like augmented reality, voice-activated assistants, and open banking are set to further alter personal finance management.
- Implementing tech-savvy budgeting needs a step-by-step approach, from assessing your financial situation to regularly reviewing and adjusting your digital budget.
- The effectiveness of budgeting tools ultimately depends on

how consistently and thoughtfully they are used.

CHAPTER 13: THE LIFESTYLE-BUDGET BALANCE - LIVING WELL WHILE STAYING ON TRACK

The concept of balancing your lifestyle with your budget is as old as money itself. From the clay tablets of ancient Babylonia to the smartphone apps of today, humans have always sought ways to manage their resources while still enjoying life. It's a dance as delicate as a tightrope walker crossing Niagara Falls, but with less dramatic consequences if you stumble (unless you're particularly unlucky with your creditors).

At it's core, the lifestyle-budget balance is about allocating your financial resources in a way that allows you to live well while still meeting your financial goals. It's not about deprivation or living like a monk (unless that's your thing, in which case, more power to you). Instead, this involves making conscious choices that align with your values and priorities.

The challenge comes from finding that sweet spot where you're not constantly stressed about money, and not blowing your entire paycheck on artisanal cheese and vintage vinyl records. It revolves around creating a sustainable financial ecosystem that can weather the storms of life while still allowing for the occasional splurge.

Historically, this balance has been achieved through various means. During the Great Depression, families used the envelope system, stuffing cash into different envelopes for different expenses. It was effective, if a bit cumbersome (and potentially risky if you had a kleptomaniac roommate).

Fast forward to the 1950s, and we see the birth of the 50/30/20 rule, which suggests allocating 50% of your income to needs, 30% to wants, and 20% to savings and debt repayment.

The Joy-to-Cost Ratio: A New Approach to Mindful Spending

Enter the Joy-to-Cost Ratio method, a modern twist on traditional budgeting that focuses on maximizing happiness while minimizing financial strain. The premise is simple: assess your expenses based on how much joy they bring you relative to their cost. It's like Marie Kondo for your wallet, but instead of asking if items spark joy, you're asking if they're worth the price tag.

Here's how it works:

1. List all your regular expenses and purchases.
2. Rate each item's 'joy factor' on a scale of 1-10.
3. Calculate the cost per use or experience for each item.
4. Divide the joy factor by the cost to get the Joy-to-Cost Ratio.
5. Rank your expenses based on their ratio.
6. Identify low-ratio items and consider eliminating or reducing them.
7. Reallocate funds to high-ratio items or experiences.
8. Regularly review and adjust your spending based on this method.

This approach can be eye-opening. You might realize that your daily latte habit, while enjoyable, has a lower Joy-to-Cost Ratio than a monthly museum membership. Or that the streaming service you barely use is dragging down your financial happiness quotient.

I once applied this method to my own spending and discovered that my gym membership, which I'd been guilting myself about not using enough, actually had a surprisingly high Joy-to-Cost Ratio. The times I did go brought me so much satisfaction that it outweighed the cost, even if I wasn't a daily attendee.

On the flip side, I realized my cable TV subscription was bringing me more frustration than joy, leading to it's swift cancellation and a redirection of funds to more fulfilling activities.

Budgeting for Self-Care and Personal Development

Self-care is not about bubble baths and face masks (though those can be lovely). It's about investing in your physical, mental, and emotional well-being. This might mean allocating funds for therapy sessions, joining a yoga class, or setting aside money for regular massages if that's what keeps you sane and functioning.

Personal development is equally important. This could involve budgeting for courses, workshops, or books that help you grow personally or professionally. The key is to view these expenses not as frivolous luxuries, but as investments in yourself that can pay dividends in the form of increased happiness, productivity, and potentially even income.

Consider creating a specific 'self-improvement' category in your budget. Start small if needed - even $50 a month can go a long way if used wisely. You might be surprised at how much free or low-cost personal development content is available online, from MOOCs (Massive Open Online Courses) to podcasts and YouTube tutorials.

Traveling on a Budget Without Sacrificing Experiences

Travel is often seen as a luxury, but with some creative thinking, it can be incorporated into even the tightest budgets. The key is to focus on experiences as opposed to amenities. A five-star hotel might be nice, but does it really add that much more value to your trip than a clean, comfortable budget option?

Consider alternative accommodations like hostels, home exchanges, or couchsurfing. Not only are these options often cheaper, but they can also provide unique cultural experiences and opportunities to meet locals and fellow travelers.

Embrace slow travel. Instead of trying to cram many destinations into a short trip, spend more time in fewer places. This allows you to really immerse yourself in the local culture and often results in a more rewarding experience. Plus, it's usually easier on the wallet.

Be flexible with your travel dates and destinations. Use tools like Skyscanner's 'Everywhere' search or Google Flights' explore feature to find the best deals. Sometimes, being open to unexpected destinations can lead to the most memorable trips.

Key Idea: *The $5 Rule. When traveling, before making any purchase, ask yourself if it's worth about an hour of your travel time (assuming you make around $20-25 per hour). This helps put expenses into perspective and ensures you're spending on things that truly matter to you.*

Eco-Friendly and Sustainable Choices in Your Budget

Incorporating sustainability into your budget doesn't have to mean spending more. In fact, many eco-friendly choices can save you money in the long run. Take reusable water bottles and shopping bags, for instance. The upfront cost is quickly offset by the money saved on bottled water and plastic bag fees.

Consider the concept of 'buy it for life' - investing in high-quality, durable items that may cost more initially but last much longer than cheaper choices. This applies to everything from clothing to kitchenware. I once splurged on a high-quality cast iron skillet, and a decade later, it's still going strong while I've watched friends cycle through many non-stick pans.

Look for ways to reduce energy consumption at home. This might involve investing in LED light bulbs, a programmable thermostat, or better insulation. These upgrades often pay for themselves through reduced utility bills.

Embrace the sharing economy. Tools like car-sharing services or community tool libraries allow you to access items you need without the expense and environmental impact of ownership.

Balancing Present Enjoyment with Future Financial Security

One of the trickiest aspects of the lifestyle-budget balance is finding the right mix of present enjoyment and future security. It's tempting to adopt an 'eat, drink, and be merry' attitude, especially when retirement seems like a distant concept. But neglecting your future self is a recipe for financial stress down the line.

The key is to make saving and investing a non-negotiable part of your budget, but not at the expense of all present enjoyment. This is where the concept of 'paying yourself first' comes in handy. Before allocating money to discretionary expenses, set aside a portion for savings and investments.

Consider automating your savings to remove the temptation to spend that money elsewhere. Set up automatic transfers to your savings account or retirement fund on payday. It's much easier to adjust your lifestyle to what's left than to try to save what's left at the end of the month (which, let's face it, is often nothing).

That said, don't forget to budget for fun in the present. Life is meant to be lived, after all. The goal is to find a balance where you're securing your future without feeling deprived in the present.

Interesting Fact: *Studies have shown that spending money on experiences as opposed to material goods leads to greater happiness and life satisfaction. So when budgeting for 'fun money', consider prioritizing experiences over things.*

Adapting Your Budget to Life Changes

Life is nothing if not unpredictable. Your carefully crafted budget will need to evolve as your circumstances change. Got a promotion? Resist the urge to immediately inflate your lifestyle to match your new income. Instead, consider maintaining your current lifestyle and directing the extra money towards savings or debt repayment.

On the flip side, if you face a job loss or income reduction, be prepared to make quick adjustments. This might mean temporarily cutting back on non-essential expenses or finding creative ways to reduce your fixed costs.

Major life events like marriage, having children, or buying a home will necessitate significant budget overhauls. The key is to be proactive as opposed to reactive. If you're planning to start a family, for instance, start adjusting your budget well in advance to account for the increased expenses.

Your budget is a living document. It should be reviewed and adjusted regularly to ensure it still aligns with your current circumstances and goals.

The Psychology of Spending and Saving

Understanding the psychological factors that influence our financial decisions can be a game-changer in maintaining a healthy lifestyle-budget balance. We humans are not always rational when it comes to money, and recognizing our biases and tendencies can help us make better choices.

For instance, we tend to value immediate gratification over long-term benefits, a phenomenon known as present bias. This is why it's so easy to overspend on things that bring immediate pleasure (like that unnecessary gadget or another pair of shoes) while neglecting long-term savings.

Another common psychological trap is lifestyle inflation. As our income increases, we tend to increase our spending proportionally, a phenomenon colorfully described as 'keeping up with the Joneses'. Being aware of this tendency can help you resist the urge to automatically upgrade your lifestyle with every pay raise.

Emotional spending is another pitfall, problem, issue, problem, issue to watch out for. Using shopping as a way to boost mood or relieve stress might provide a temporary high, but it can wreak havoc on your budget. Finding non-financial ways to manage emotions, like exercise or meditation, can help stop this tendency.

On the flip side, some people experience anxiety or guilt around spending money, even on necessary items. This can lead to excessive frugality that impacts quality of life. If this sounds like you, it might be helpful to reframe spending as an investment in your well-being and happiness, not just an outflow of money.

The Role of Financial Education

Improving your financial literacy can go a long way in helping you maintain a healthy lifestyle-budget balance. The more you understand about personal finance, the better equipped you'll be to make informed decisions about your money.

This doesn't mean you need to become a financial expert overnight. Start small - read personal finance blogs, listen to money-focused podcasts, or pick up a book on budgeting. Many banks and credit unions offer free financial education resources to their customers.

Consider using budgeting apps or software to help you track your spending and stay on top of your finances. These tools can provide valuable insights into your spending patterns and help you identify areas where you might be able to cut back. The goal of financial education isn't to turn you into a penny-pinching miser, but to empower you to make choices that align with your values and goals. It's about using money as a tool to create the life you want, as opposed to letting money control your life.

Key Takeaways

- The lifestyle-budget balance is about aligning your spending with your values and priorities, not deprivation.
- Use the Joy-to-Cost Ratio method to assess and improve your spending.
- Invest in self-care and personal development as part of your budget.
- Travel smartly by focusing on experiences over luxury and being flexible with plans.
- Incorporate eco-friendly choices into your budget - they often save money in the long run.
- Balance present enjoyment with future security by automating savings and investing.
- Adapt your budget to life changes proactively.
- Understand the psychology behind your financial decisions to make better choices.
- Continuously educate yourself about personal finance to improve your financial decision making skills.

CHAPTER 14: BEYOND BUDGETING - ACHIEVING FINANCIAL FREEDOM

Financial freedom. It's the holy grail of personal finance, the pot of gold at the end of the budgeting rainbow.

But How would you feel if I shared with you that the path to this promised land isn't paved with spreadsheets and penny-pinching? Welcome to the world beyond budgeting, where the air is fresh, the grass is greener, and your wallet isn't constantly on a diet.

For years, we've been fed the idea that strict budgeting is the only way to financial salvation. We've dutifully tracked every penny, agonized over every purchase, and treated our bank accounts like temperamental toddlers that need constant supervision.

But here's what's interesting: while budgeting is a useful tool, it's not the be-all and end-all of financial success.

The concept of financial freedom has evolved. It's no longer just about having enough money to retire comfortably.

It's about creating a life where work is optional, where your money works harder than you do, and where you have the freedom to pursue your passions without constantly checking your bank balance.

This shift in thinking isn't just a pipe dream cooked up by millennials sipping overpriced lattes. It's a movement that's gaining traction across generations, fueled by changing attitudes towards work, life, and the pursuit of happiness.

The FIRE (Financial Independence, Retire Early) movement, which gained popularity in the 2010s, is just one manifestation of this new approach to financial planning. And trust me, it's a lot more fun than balancing spreadsheets.

The New Face of Financial Freedom

Financial freedom isn't about having a specific number in your bank account. It's about having options. It's the ability to say "no" to things that don't align with your values and "yes" to opportunities that excite you. It's about creating a life that's rich in experiences, not just in dollars and cents.

This new definition of financial freedom is deeply personal. For some, it might mean the ability to travel the world without worrying about a paycheck. For others, it could be the freedom to start a business or pursue a creative passion. And for many, it's simply the peace of mind that comes from knowing you're not one unexpected expense away from financial ruin.

The concept of 'work optional' has gained particular traction in recent years, especially in the wake of the COVID-19 pandemic. People are increasingly questioning the traditional 9-to-5 grind and seeking ways to decouple their income from their time. This doesn't necessarily mean never working again – this involves having the choice to work on your own terms.

Passive income is the not-so-secret weapon in this new approach to financial freedom. It's the idea of creating income streams that need minimal ongoing effort to maintain. This could be through investments, rental properties, online businesses, or even creative endeavors like writing books or creating online courses. The goal is to build multiple income streams that can support your lifestyle without requiring you to trade your time for money constantly.

But here's the rub: achieving this kind of financial freedom requires a shift in mindset. It's more than just saving more or earning more (although those things certainly help). It's about fundamentally changing your relationship with money and work.

Rewriting Your Financial Story

The first step in moving beyond budgeting is to rewrite your financial story. We all have narratives about money that we've inherited from our parents, society, or our own experiences. These stories shape our behaviors and beliefs about what's possible for us financially.

Maybe you grew up believing that money is scarce and hard to come by. Or perhaps you've internalized the idea that you're "bad with money." These limiting beliefs can hold you back from achieving true financial freedom, no matter how meticulously you budget. Changing these narratives isn't easy, but it's essential. Start by examining your beliefs about money. Where did they come from? Are they serving you? If not, it's time to consciously choose new beliefs that align with your vision of financial freedom.

For instance, instead of thinking "I'll never have enough money," try reframing it as "I'm constantly finding new ways to increase my income and build wealth." This isn't just positive thinking mumbo-jumbo – this involves creating a mindset that opens you up to opportunities and motivates you to take action.

The Art of Strategic Spending

Moving beyond budgeting doesn't mean throwing caution to the wind and spending with abandon. It means being strategic about your spending in a way that aligns with your values and long-term goals. Instead of obsessing over every small expense, focus on optimizing your big three: housing, transportation, and food. These categories typically make up the bulk of most people's expenses. By making smart choices in these areas, you can free up a significant amount of money without feeling deprived.

For housing, this might mean house hacking (renting out part of your home to offset your mortgage) or choosing to live in a more affordable area. With transportation, it could be opting for a reliable used car instead of a new one, or using public transportation when possible. And for food, learning to cook and meal prep can save you thousands over eating out regularly.

The key is to be intentional about your spending. Before making a purchase, ask yourself: Does this align with my values and goals? Will it bring me closer to financial freedom? If the answer is no, it's probably not worth it, no matter how good the deal seems.

Building Your Freedom Fund

While we're moving beyond traditional budgeting, that doesn't mean we're abandoning the concept of saving altogether. Instead, we're reframing it as building your "freedom fund." Your freedom fund is the pool of money that will eventually give you the option to work on your own terms. It's more than just retirement – this involves creating flexibility and options in your life now and in the future.

The traditional advice of saving 10-15% of your income is a good starting point, but if you're serious about achieving financial freedom sooner rather than later, you'll want to aim higher. Many proponents of the FIRE movement advocate saving 50% or more of their income. Now, I know what you're thinking. "50%? Are you out of your mind?" But hear me out. This level of saving doesn't have to mean living like a monk. It's about being creative and finding ways to increase your savings rate without sacrificing your quality of life.

This might mean finding ways to increase your income through side hustles or negotiating a raise at work. It could involve house hacking or geo-arbitrage (moving to a lower cost of living area while maintaining your income). The specific strategies will depend on your situation, but the goal is to create as big a gap as possible between your income and your expenses.

The Power of Passive Income

Remember how we talked about passive income earlier? Well, it's time to explore further into this magical realm where money grows while you sleep (or while you're binge-watching your favorite show – no judgment here).

Passive income is the secret sauce that can accelerate your path to financial freedom. It's what allows you to break free from the time-for-money trap and start building wealth exponentially.

There are countless ways to generate passive income, but here are a few popular options:

1. Real estate investing: This could involve buying rental properties or investing in real estate investment trusts (REITs).
2. Dividend-paying stocks: Companies that pay regular dividends can provide a steady stream of passive income.
3. Creating digital products: E-books, online courses, or stock photography can continue to generate income long after the initial work is done.
4. Peer-to-peer lending: Platforms like Prosper or LendingClub allow you to earn interest by lending money to people or businesses.
5. Building a business: While not entirely passive at first, a well-structured business can eventually run with minimal input from you.

The key is to start small and diversify. Don't put all your eggs in one passive income basket. Experiment with different strategies and see what works best for you.

The Role of Financial Education

Now, I'm about to say something that might shock you: financial education is more important than budgeting. There, I said it. Call the personal finance police if you must, but hear me out first. You see, budgeting is a tactical skill. It's useful, sure, but it's limited.

Financial education, on the other hand, is strategic. It gives you the knowledge and tools to make better financial decisions across all areas of your life. Financial education is not about learning how to balance a checkbook or calculate compound interest (although those are useful skills). It revolves around understanding how money works in the real world. It involves learning to think like an investor, not just a consumer.

This kind of education can come from books, podcasts, courses, or even mentors who have achieved the kind of financial freedom you're aiming for. The important thing is to make learning about money a lifelong habit. And here's the beautiful thing: as you become more financially educated, you'll find that strict budgeting becomes less necessary. You'll naturally make better financial decisions because you understand the long-term implications of your choices.

Creating Your Personal Financial Philosophy

As you move beyond budgeting and towards true financial freedom, it's crucial to develop your own personal financial philosophy. This is the set of principles that will guide your financial decisions and keep you on track towards your goals. Your financial philosophy should reflect your values and priorities. It's not about following someone else's rules, but about creating a framework that works for you.

Here are some questions to consider as you develop your financial philosophy:

- What does financial freedom mean to you?
- What are your core values, and how do they relate to money?

- What role do you want money to play in your life?
- How much is "enough" for you?
- What are you willing to sacrifice (or not sacrifice) to achieve your financial goals?

There's no one-size-fits-all approach to personal finance. What works for someone else might not work for you, and that's okay. The goal is to create a philosophy that aligns with your unique goals and circumstances.

The Psychology of Financial Freedom

Let's talk about the elephant in the room: the psychological aspect of financial freedom. Because let's face it, if achieving financial freedom were purely a matter of math, we'd all be sipping piña coladas on our private islands by now.

Our emotions and psychological quirks play a huge role in our financial lives. Fear, greed, impulsivity, and even our self-image can all impact our financial decisions. One of the biggest psychological hurdles to overcome is the scarcity mindset. This is the belief that there's never enough money, time, or resources to go around. It's the voice in your head that says, "I can't afford that" or "I'll never have enough."

The scarcity mindset can keep you stuck in a cycle of financial stress and poor decision-making. It can lead to overspending (because you feel like you need to grab opportunities while you can) or under-investing (because you're too afraid to take risks).

The antidote to the scarcity mindset is abundance thinking. This doesn't mean being unrealistic or ignoring financial realities. It means recognizing that there are always opportunities to grow, learn, and improve your financial situation.

Abundance thinking allows you to see possibilities where others see limitations. It encourages creativity and problem-solving. And perhaps most importantly, it helps you maintain a sense of optimism and resilience on your path to financial freedom.

Navigating the Bumps in the Road

Now, I'd love to tell you that the path to financial freedom is all sunshine and roses, but let's get real for a moment. Life has a funny way of throwing curveballs when you least expect them. Maybe you lose your job, face a health crisis, or find yourself in the middle of a global pandemic (because apparently, that's a thing now). These unexpected events can derail even the best-laid financial plans.

The key is to build resilience into your financial strategy. This means having multiple income streams, maintaining an emergency fund, and being flexible in your approach. It also means being prepared to adjust your timeline. Financial freedom isn't a race – it's a journey.

If you hit a setback, it doesn't mean you've failed. It just means you need to recalibrate and keep moving forward. Financial freedom isn't about perfection. It's about progress. Every step you take towards your goals, no matter how small, is a victory worth celebrating.

Key Takeaways

- Financial freedom is about creating options and aligning your finances with your values.
- Moving beyond budgeting requires a shift in mindset and a focus on strategic spending.
- Building multiple streams of passive income is key to achieving work-optional status.
- Continuous financial education is more valuable than strict budgeting in the long run.
- Developing a personal financial philosophy helps guide decisions and maintain focus.
- Addressing the psychological aspects of money is crucial for long-term success.
- Building financial resilience helps navigate unexpected challenges.
- The attainment of financial freedom is about progress, not perfection.

CHAPTER 15: MAINTAINING MOMENTUM - KEEPING YOUR BUDGET ALIVE AND THRIVING

Most of us start budgeting with the best intentions. We meticulously track every penny, swear off unnecessary purchases, and vow to transform our financial lives overnight. But let's face it, maintaining that initial burst of enthusiasm is about as easy as resisting a second slice of chocolate cake at a birthday party.

Before long, our once pristine budget becomes a neglected relic, gathering digital dust in some forgotten corner of our computer. I'll admit, I've been there. My first try at budgeting lasted about as long as my New Year's resolution to hit the gym five times a week. By February, both my budget and my unused gym membership were quietly mocking me from afar.

It wasn't until I stumbled upon the concept of budget maintenance that I realized the key to financial success isn't just creating a budget – it's keeping it alive and kicking. Think of your budget as a garden. You wouldn't plant a bunch of seeds, walk away, and expect a thriving vegetable patch three months later.

No, you'd water it regularly, pull out the weeds, and adjust your approach based on what's growing well and what's withering on the vine. Your budget needs the same level of care and attention.

But here's what's interesting – maintaining your budget doesn't have to be a soul-crushing chore. In fact, with the right approach, it can be downright invigorating.

Invigorating. Like the feeling you get after organizing your sock drawer or finally tackling that mountain of dishes in the sink. There's a certain satisfaction in knowing you're on top of your financial game, and that's exactly what we're aiming for. We're about to begin on a journey to improve your budget from a wilting wallflower into the life of the financial party. And trust me, it's going to be a lot more fun than you think.

The Art of the Regular Review

The cornerstone of maintaining budget momentum is the regular review. Now, I know what you're thinking. "Regular review" sounds about as exciting as watching paint dry.

But hear me out. These reviews are your chance to play financial detective, uncovering the mysteries of where your money's really going and plotting your course to financial freedom. Aim for a monthly review at minimum. Set a specific date – say, the first Saturday of every month – and treat it like an important appointment. Because it is. This is your date with financial destiny, guys. Make it special. Pour yourself a fancy beverage, put on some music, and settle in for some quality time with your numbers.

During your review, you'll want to compare your actual spending to your budgeted amounts. Did you stick to your grocery budget, or did those late-night ice cream runs add up more than you realized? How about that "miscellaneous" category that somehow always seems to balloon out of control? This is your chance to face the music and adjust your symphony accordingly.

But don't just look at the numbers. Reflect on the why behind your spending. That $50 you dropped on a new plant might seem frivolous at first glance, but if it brightened up your home office and boosted your productivity, it might be worth every penny. On the flip side, that subscription box you forgot to cancel? Not so much.

Use your review to make necessary adjustments. Maybe you consistently overspend in one category and underspend in another. This is your chance to reallocate funds and make your budget work for your real life, not some idealized version of it. A budget that doesn't reflect reality is about as useful as a chocolate teapot.

Key Idea: *Your budget is a living document, not a set-it-and-forget-it tool. Regular reviews keep it relevant and effective.*

Yes, you heard me right. We're going to talk about throwing parties for your money. Well, sort of. You see, maintaining momentum isn't about crunching numbers and tightening belts. It's about acknowledging your progress and giving yourself a well-deserved pat on the back. Or a slice of cake. Or both. I'm not here to judge.

Set specific, achievable milestones for yourself. Maybe it's saving your first $1,000 emergency fund, or paying off a particular debt, or going a whole month without buying clothes you don't need. Whatever it is, when you hit that milestone, celebrate it. And I mean really celebrate it.

When I paid off my student loans, I threw myself a "Debt-Free Degree" party. I invited friends over, made a cake decorated like a diploma, and we toasted to financial freedom. Was it a bit cheesy? Absolutely. Did it make me feel like a financial superhero? You bet your bottom dollar it did.

These celebrations serve a dual purpose. First, they give you a much-needed morale boost. Budgeting can sometimes feel like an endless slog, and these moments of joy remind you why you're doing it in the first place. Second, they create positive associations with good financial habits. Your brain starts to link the pleasure of celebration with the act of saving or paying off debt, making you more likely to stick to your goals.

But here's the catch – make sure your celebrations don't derail your budget. A $500 shopping spree to celebrate saving $500 kind of defeats the purpose, doesn't it? Get creative with low-cost ways to mark your achievements. A picnic in the park, a movie night at home, or even just bragging rights on social media can do the trick.

Weathering the Storms: Handling Budget Setbacks

Life has a funny way of throwing financial curveballs when we least expect them. Your car decides to break down the same week your dog needs emergency surgery, and suddenly your carefully crafted budget is in shambles. It's enough to make you want to throw in the towel and declare budgeting bankruptcy. But hold your horses, partner. We're not going down without a fight.

The first step in handling budget setbacks is to take a deep breath. Seriously. Take a moment to remind yourself that setbacks are a normal part of the financial journey. You haven't failed - you've just encountered a plot twist in your money story.

Next, assess the damage. How far off course has this setback thrown you? Is it a minor blip or a major derailment? Once you have a clear picture of the situation, you can start formulating your comeback plan.

If it's a minor setback, you might be able to course-correct by tightening your belt in other areas for a month or two. Maybe you eat out less or postpone that new gadget purchase. Think of it as a financial detour – you're still heading to the same destination, just taking a slightly different route.

For major setbacks, you might need to revisit your overall budget strategy. This could mean temporarily pausing some savings goals or looking for ways to increase your income. It's okay to shift gears when circumstances change. Flexibility is the name of the game.

One of the most infuential resources in your setback-handling arsenal is your emergency fund. This is why we harp on about having one. It's your financial airbag, cushioning the blow when life decides to play bumper cars with your budget. If you've had to dip into your emergency fund, make replenishing it a priority once you're back on your feet.

Key Insight: *Setbacks are not failures - they're opportunities to refine your budget and strengthen your financial resilience.*

The Accountability Alliance: Your Secret Weapon for Staying on Track

Now, let's talk about something that might make you squirm a little: accountability. I know, I know. The mere thought of sharing your financial goals with someone else might make you break out in a cold sweat.

But hear me out, because this might just be the game-changer you've been looking for. Enter the Accountability Alliance. This isn't some fancy financial product or a complex budgeting technique. It's simply the act of partnering up with someone – a friend, family member, or even a like-minded stranger from a personal finance forum – to keep each other on track with your financial goals.

Here's how it works: You and your accountability partner share your financial goals and agree to check in regularly – say, once a month. During these check-ins, you talk about your progress, challenges, and any adjustments you've made to your budget. You celebrate each other's wins and brainstorm solutions for obstacles.

The beauty of the Accountability Alliance comes from it's simplicity and effectiveness. When you know someone else is expecting an update on your progress, you're more likely to stay committed to your goals. It's the financial equivalent of having a gym buddy – you're less likely to skip leg day when you know your friend is waiting for you at the squat rack.

But the benefits go beyond just keeping you accountable. Your partner can offer a fresh perspective on your financial challenges, suggest solutions you might not have thought of, and provide emotional support when the budgeting journey gets tough.

Plus, there's something incredibly motivating about celebrating your wins with someone who truly understands the effort behind them. When choosing an accountability partner, look for someone who shares your commitment to financial improvement but perhaps has different strengths or experiences. Maybe they're a whiz at finding creative ways to save money, while you excel at increasing your income.

Together, you can learn from each other and grow your financial skills. Vulnerability is key here. Be honest about your struggles and setbacks. The more open you are, the more your partner can help you. And who knows? Your honesty might just inspire them to open up about their own financial hurdles.

The Never-Ending Story: Continuous Financial Education

If you think you can learn everything there is to know about personal finance in one go, I've got a bridge to sell you. Think of it as cross-training for your financial muscles. The more you know, the better equipped you'll be to make informed decisions and adapt your budget to changing circumstances.

But before you start having flashbacks to high school economics class, let me assure you – this doesn't have to be a snooze-fest. Financial education can be as entertaining as it is informative.

Here are some painless ways to keep your money knowledge fresh:

1. **Podcasts**: Listen to financial podcasts during your commute or while doing chores. It's like eavesdropping on money experts, minus the awkwardness of actually eavesdropping.
2. **Books**: Pick up a personal finance book (besides this one). Many are written in a conversational, engaging style that's a far cry from dry textbooks. My personal favorite? "The Richest Man in Babylon." It's basically financial advice disguised as a series of parables set in ancient Babylon. Who knew budgeting could be so... epic?

3. **Blogs and Online Forums**: Follow reputable financial blogs or join online communities. It's like having a team of money-savvy friends at your fingertips, minus the obligation to remember their birthdays.
4. **Courses**: Take a free online course on a specific financial topic. Websites like Coursera and edX offer university-level courses without the university-level price tag.
5. **Gamification**: Try financial literacy apps that turn learning about money into a game. Because who says budgeting can't come with power-ups and boss levels?

The key is to make financial education a regular part of your routine. Set aside a little time each week to learn something new. Maybe it's "Finance Friday," where you spend 30 minutes reading a money blog or listening to a podcast. Or perhaps it's "Money Monday," where you tackle one module of an online course.

The goal isn't to become a financial guru overnight. It's to gradually build your knowledge and confidence over time. Each little bit of information you absorb is another tool in your financial toolkit, ready to be deployed when the need arises.

Fun Fact: The concept of budgeting dates back to ancient civilizations. The Babylonians used clay tablets to track their income and expenses over 7,000 years ago. And you thought your Excel spreadsheet was old school!

The Momentum Maximizer Method: Your Step-by-Step Guide

Alright, troops. It's time to put all this knowledge into action with the Momentum Maximizer Method. This isn't just another budgeting technique – it's a comprehensive approach to keeping your financial mojo flowing.

Let's break it down:

1. **Schedule Monthly Money Dates**: Set a recurring appointment with yourself (and your accountability partner, if you have one) for a monthly budget review. Make it official – put it in your calendar, set a reminder, maybe even buy yourself a special "money date" mug for the occasion.
2. **Track Daily, Review Weekly**: Use a method that works for you – an app, a spreadsheet, or good old pen and paper – to track your expenses daily. Then, do a quick weekly check-in. This keeps you aware of your spending patterns without becoming obsessive.
3. **Analyze and Adjust**: During your monthly review, dig deep into your spending patterns. Are there any surprises? Any areas where you consistently over or underspend? Use this information to tweak your budget categories as needed.
4. **Set Specific Monthly Goals**: Each month, set one or two specific, measurable financial goals. Maybe it's to cut your takeout spending by 20% or to put an extra $100 towards your debt. Having a clear target keeps you focused and motivated.
5. **Celebrate Wins, Big and Small**: Did you meet your monthly goal? Celebrate! Did you resist an impulse purchase? That's worth a little victory dance too. Acknowledging your progress, no matter how small, keeps your momentum going.
6. **Address Overspending Immediately**: If you notice you're overspending in a category, don't wait until the end of the month to address it. Make adjustments on the fly to keep yourself on track.
7. **Continuous Learning**: Commit to learning one new financial concept or skill each month. Maybe this month you learn about index funds, and next month you dive into the mysteries of credit scores.

8. **Quarterly Big-Picture Review**: Every three months, zoom out and look at the big picture. How are you progressing towards your long-term financial goals? Do these goals still align with your values and life situation?
9. **Annual Budget Overhaul**: Once a year, do a finish review and refresh of your budget. This is your chance to make big changes based on what you've learned over the past year.
10. **Rinse and Repeat**: Keep this cycle going, adjusting as needed. The goal is progress, not perfection.

The issues of Perfection: Avoiding Budget Burnout

Now, let's address the other elephant in the room – the pursuit of the perfect budget. It's a noble goal, but about as achievable as finding a unicorn in your backyard. Striving for budgeting perfection is a surefire way to burn yourself out faster than a candle in a windstorm.

One of the biggest pitfalls, problems, issues, problems, issues is obsessive tracking. Yes, knowing where your money goes is important, but if you're spending hours each day logging every penny, you're setting yourself up for frustration.

It's like trying to count every grain of sand on the beach – exhausting and ultimately pointless. Instead, focus on the big picture. Use tools that make tracking easier, like apps that automatically categorize your spending. And remember, it's okay if things aren't 100% accurate all the time. As long as you're in the ballpark, you're doing fine.

Another common pitfall, problem, issue, problem, issue is the all-or-nothing mentality. You overspend one day, and suddenly you feel like you've failed completely. Before you know it, you're on a financial bender, buying everything in sight because "you've already blown the budget anyway." This, my friends, is what we call the "what-the-hell effect," and this involves as helpful as a screen door on a submarine.

Budgeting is not about perfection – this involves progress. If you overspend one day, it's not the end of the world. Acknowledge it, learn from it, and move on. Your budget is there to guide you, not to punish you.

Lastly, beware of comparison-itis. In this age of social media, it's easy to fall into the trap of comparing your financial journey to others. But here's the thing – you're seeing their highlight reel, not their behind-the-scenes footage.

For all you know, that friend bragging about their amazing investments might be up to their eyeballs in credit card debt. Focus on your own progress. Celebrate your wins, learn from your setbacks, and keep moving forward. Your financial journey is unique to you, and that's what makes it beautiful.

Adapting Your Budget: Because Life Happens

Life has a funny way of throwing curveballs when we least expect them. One day you're cruising along with your perfectly balanced budget, and the next you're facing a job loss, a surprise medical bill, or hey, maybe even a global pandemic. (Too soon?)

The key to maintaining momentum in the face of life's surprises is adaptability. Your budget should be flexible enough to bend without breaking.

Here are some strategies for adapting your budget to different scenarios:

1. **Income Changes**: If your income increases, resist the urge to immediately inflate your lifestyle. Instead, allocate a portion to your financial goals and a portion to improving your quality of life. If your income decreases, prioritize your essential expenses and look for areas to cut back temporarily.
2. **Major Life Events**: Getting married? Having a baby? Moving to a new city? These life changes often come with significant financial implications. Take the time to sit down and reassess your budget from the ground up. You might need to create entirely new categories or significantly adjust existing ones.
3. **Seasonal Variations**: Many expenses fluctuate seasonally. Your heating bill might skyrocket in winter, or you might spend more on social activities in summer. Plan for these variations by setting up sinking funds – small amounts you save each month for specific future expenses.
4. **Economic Changes**: Keep an eye on broader economic trends that might affect your finances. Rising inflation might mean you need to adjust your grocery budget. A recession might prompt you to beef up your emergency fund.
5. **Changing Goals**: As you progress on your financial journey, your goals might change. Maybe you've paid off your debt and now want to focus on investing. Or perhaps you've decided to save for a house instead of extensive travel. Regularly reassess your goals and adjust your budget to align with your current priorities.

Adapting your budget doesn't mean throwing it out the window. It revolves around making thoughtful adjustments that allow you to stay on track with your long-term financial goals while dealing with short-term changes.

Key Takeaway: A good budget is like a willow tree – strong enough to withstand storms, but flexible enough to bend with the wind.

Key Takeaways

- Regular budget reviews are crucial for maintaining financial momentum. Treat them like important appointments with yourself.
- Celebrate your financial milestones, both big and small. It keeps you motivated and creates positive associations with good money habits.
- Setbacks are normal. Handle them by assessing the damage, adjusting your plan, and getting back on track.
- The Accountability Alliance can be a powerful tool for staying committed to your financial goals.
- Continuous financial education is key to adapting your budget to changing circumstances and making informed decisions.
- The Momentum Maximizer Method provides a structured approach to keeping your budget alive and thriving.
- Avoid the pitfalls, problems, issues, problems, issues of perfectionism. Focus on progress, not perfection.
- Adaptability is crucial. Your budget should be flexible enough to handle life's curveballs.
- Maintaining budget momentum is a marathon, not a sprint. Stay consistent, stay flexible, and keep your eye on the prize.

CONCLUSION: YOUR FINANCIAL TRANSFORMATION STARTS NOW

I've always found it amusing how we treat money like it's some mystical force beyond our control. We moan about our empty bank accounts as if they were cursed by an ancient deity, rather than the result of our own spending habits. But here's what's interesting: your financial situation is not a cosmic joke played on you by the universe. It's the sum total of your choices, habits, and yes, even your mindset.

You might be thinking, "Great, another lecture about pinching pennies and giving up my daily latte." But that's not what this involves. This is about empowerment, about taking the reins of your financial life and steering it in the direction you want to go. It's about creating a personalized action plan that doesn't just look good on paper, but actually works in the messy reality of your life.

Financial wellness isn't about having a fat bank account (though that certainly doesn't hurt). It's about the ripple effect that financial stability creates in every aspect of your life. When you're not constantly stressed about money, you sleep better.

When you're not living paycheck to paycheck, you have the freedom to pursue opportunities that truly excite you. When you have a solid financial foundation, your relationships improve because money stops being a source of constant tension.

So, let's roll up our sleeves and get down to the nitty-gritty of transforming your financial life. No more vague promises or pie-in-the-sky dreams. We're talking concrete steps, real-world strategies, and a hefty dose of motivation to keep you going when the going gets tough.

The Ripple Effect of Financial Wellness

Financial wellness isn't about numbers on a spreadsheet. It's about the profound impact it has on every facet of your life. When you achieve a state of financial well-being, it's like dropping a pebble in a pond – the effects ripple outward, touching areas of your life you might not have even considered.

Let's start with the obvious: stress reduction. Financial stress is like a constant background noise, always humming in your ears, making it hard to focus on anything else. When you get your finances under control, that noise fades away. Suddenly, you can hear yourself think again. You're not constantly doing mental math, trying to figure out if you can afford groceries this week.

This reduction in stress has tangible health benefits. Your blood pressure goes down, your sleep improves, and you might even find those stress-induced headaches becoming a thing of the past. Your relationships improve too. Money is one of the leading causes of arguments in relationships. When you and your partner are on the same financial page, working towards shared goals, it creates a sense of teamwork and mutual support. You're no longer playing the blame game every time a bill comes due. Instead, you're celebrating your financial wins together, big and small.

Your career can also get a boost from financial wellness. When you're not desperately clinging to a job you hate just for the paycheck, you have the freedom to take risks, to pursue opportunities that align with your passions and values. Maybe you've always wanted to start your own business, but the fear of financial instability held you back. With a solid financial foundation, you can take that leap with confidence.

Even your leisure time becomes more enjoyable. When you've budgeted for fun and know you can afford it, you can truly relax and enjoy yourself without that nagging guilt in the back of your mind. Your vacations become times of genuine relaxation and rejuvenation, not just another source of financial stress.

Key Insight: *Financial wellness isn't about money – this involves creating a life of reduced stress, improved relationships, career freedom, and guilt-free enjoyment.*

Creating Your Personalized Action Plan

Now, let's get down to brass tacks. Creating a personalized action plan is not a one-size-fits-all affair. Your financial situation is as unique as your fingerprint, and your plan should reflect that. But don't worry, I'm not going to leave you hanging with vague advice. We're going to break this down into actionable steps that you can start implementing today.

First things first: you need to get brutally honest with yourself about where you stand financially. This means taking a hard look at your income, expenses, debts, and assets. I know it's tempting to bury your head in the sand, but trust me, knowledge is power here.

Pull out those bank statements, credit card bills, and investment reports. Spreadsheets are your friends in this process. Create a comprehensive overview of your financial life. It might not be pretty, but it's the only way to know where you're starting from.

Once you have a clear picture of your current situation, it's time to set some goals. And I'm not talking about vague aspirations like "be rich" or "stop being broke." We need specific, measurable, achievable, relevant, and time-bound (SMART) goals. Maybe you want to pay off your credit card debt in 18 months. Or save $10,000 for a down payment on a house in two years. Whatever your goals are, write them down. There's something powerful about putting your goals on paper – it makes them real, tangible.

Now comes the part that many people dread: creating a budget. But here's the thing – a budget isn't a financial straitjacket. It's a roadmap to your goals. Start by tracking your expenses for a month. Every single penny. You might be surprised (or horrified) to see where your money is actually going.

Once you have this information, you can start making informed decisions about where to cut back and where to allocate more funds. The 50/30/20 rule can be a good starting point for many people. This means allocating 50% of your income to needs (like housing, food, and utilities), 30% to wants (entertainment, dining out), and 20% to savings and debt repayment. But remember, this is just a guideline. Your personal situation might require a different breakdown.

One of the most crucial aspects of your action plan is automating your finances as much as possible. Set up automatic transfers to your savings account on payday. Use apps to track your spending. Set up automatic bill payments to avoid late fees. The less you have to actively think about and manage your money on a day-to-day basis, the more likely you are to stick to your plan.

Don't forget to build in some flexibility and fun money into your plan. If your budget is too restrictive, you're setting yourself up for failure. It's like going on a crash diet – you might see some quick results, but it's not sustainable in the long run.

Allow yourself some wiggle room for unexpected expenses and small indulgences.

Finally, commit to regular check-ins with yourself. Set aside time each month to review your progress, celebrate your wins (no matter how small), and adjust your plan as needed. Your financial situation will change over time, and your plan should evolve with it.

The Financial Wellness Ripple Effect: A Step-by-Step Guide

1. **Face the Music**: Pull out all your financial statements and create a comprehensive overview of your current situation. Knowledge is power, even if it's uncomfortable at first.
2. **Dream Big, Plan Smart**: Set SMART goals that excite and motivate you. Write them down and put them somewhere you'll see them every day.
3. **Map Your Money**: Create a budget that aligns with your goals. Use the 50/30/20 rule as a starting point, but adjust as needed for your personal situation.
4. **Automate for Success**: Set up automatic transfers, bill payments, and use apps to track your spending. The less you have to actively manage, the better.
5. **Build Your Safety Net**: Start with an emergency fund. Aim for 3-6 months of living expenses. This will give you peace of mind and financial flexibility.
6. **Tackle Debt Strategically**: If you have high-interest debt, make paying it off a priority. Consider the debt avalanche method (paying off highest interest debt first) or the debt snowball method (paying off smallest debts first for psychological wins).
7. **Invest in Your Future**: Once you have your emergency fund and high-interest debt under control, start investing for

the long term. Take advantage of any employer-matched retirement contributions.
8. **Educate Yourself**: Make financial literacy a lifelong pursuit. Read books, listen to podcasts, attend workshops. The more you know, the better decisions you'll make.
9. **Find Your Tribe**: Surround yourself with people who support your financial goals. Consider joining or starting a money mastermind group for accountability and support.
10. **Celebrate Your Wins**: Acknowledge your progress, no matter how small. Each step forward is a victory worth celebrating.

Avoiding Common issues

Even with the best-laid plans, there are always potential pitfalls, problems, issues, problems, issues along the way. But forewarned is forearmed, as they say. Let's talk about some common stumbling blocks and how to sidestep them.

One of the biggest pitfalls, problems, issues, problems, issues is the "all or nothing" mentality. You might think that if you can't follow your budget perfectly, you might as well give up entirely. This kind of black-and-white thinking is a recipe for failure.

Financial wellness is not about perfection – this involves progress. If you slip up (and you will, because you're human), don't beat yourself up. Acknowledge it, learn from it, and get back on track.

Another common issue is lifestyle inflation. As your income increases, it's tempting to increase your spending proportionally. Suddenly, things that were once luxuries become "necessities." Before you know it, you're living paycheck to paycheck despite earning more than ever. Combat this by consciously deciding how much of any income increase you'll save or invest before you start spending it.

Comparison is another trap that can derail your financial progress. In this age of social media, it's all too easy to fall into the comparison game. Those carefully curated Instagram posts don't show the whole picture. Focus on your own goals and progress, not someone else's highlight reel.

Emotional spending can also throw a wrench in your financial plans. Whether you're celebrating a win or trying to cheer yourself up after a bad day, using shopping as an emotional crutch can quickly undo your hard work. Find other ways to process your emotions – go for a run, call a friend, or practice meditation.

Finally, don't fall into the trap of thinking that budgeting means you can never have fun or enjoy life. This kind of restrictive thinking is not sustainable. Instead, build fun and enjoyment into your budget. Plan for it, save for it, and then enjoy it guilt-free.

Adapting Your Plan for Life's Curveballs

Life has a funny way of throwing curveballs when we least expect them. Your financial plan needs to be flexible enough to adapt to these changes without completely derailing your progress. Major life events like marriage, divorce, having children, or changing careers can significantly impact your financial situation. When these events occur, take the time to reassess your goals and adjust your plan accordingly. Don't be afraid to completely overhaul your budget if necessary.

Economic downturns or unexpected job loss can also throw a wrench in your plans. This is where having an emergency fund becomes crucial. If you find yourself in this situation, focus on cutting non-essential expenses and look for ways to increase your income, even temporarily. On the flip side, windfalls like inheritances or large bonuses require careful planning too. It's tempting to see this as "free money" and splurge, but this is an opportunity to fast-track your financial goals. Consider putting a significant portion towards debt repayment or investments.

Health issues can also impact your financial plan. This is why having adequate insurance coverage is so important. Regularly review your health, life, and disability insurance to confirm you're adequately protected.

Adapting your plan doesn't mean you've failed. It means you're responsive and realistic about the changing circumstances of your life. Flexibility is a strength, not a weakness, when it comes to long-term financial wellness.

Key Takeaway: Your financial plan should be a living document, regularly reviewed and adjusted to reflect the changing circumstances of your life. Flexibility and adaptability are key to long-term financial success.

Key Takeaways

- Financial wellness has a ripple effect, positively impacting your stress levels, relationships, career, and overall life satisfaction.
- Creating a personalized action plan involves honest assessment, setting SMART goals, budgeting, and automating your finances.
- Regular check-ins and adjustments are crucial for long-term success.

- Common pitfalls, problems, issues, problems, issues include all-or-nothing thinking, lifestyle inflation, comparison, and emotional spending.
- Your financial plan should be flexible enough to adapt to major life changes and unexpected events.
- Celebrate your progress, no matter how small, and remember that financial wellness is about progress, not perfection.
- Continuous financial education and surrounding yourself with supportive people can significantly boost your chances of success.
- Building fun and enjoyment into your budget is essential for long-term sustainability.
- An emergency fund is crucial for weathering life's unexpected challenges.
- Your financial transformation starts now – take that first step today.

www.ingramcontent.com/pod-product-compliance
Lightning Source LLC
Chambersburg PA
CBHW071026240526
45469CB00006BD/2108